"The essays in this collection under from page to page in order to und place, heritage, art, and gender—and a levee-breaking flood that then makes a consciousness. Along the way, Chachi Hauser guides us through New Orleans underground parties, eerie Disney re-constructions, and painful breakups, all with a steely inquiry and a deeply-feeling narrative. *It's Fun to Be a Person I Don't Know* is a wonderful collection that introduces a noteworthy voice to the American essay form."

—ELENA PASSARELLO, author of *Animals Strike Curious Poses*

"What separates us from others and how intrinsically connected are we, for better or worse? Chachi Hauser's collection *It's Fun to Be a Person I Don't Know* goes head-to-head with these large and ancient philosophical considerations, with bravado, intimacy, and unwavering curiosity. Simultaneously sensitive and fearless, Hauser's work explores expectations, assumptions, and discoveries about what family history is, and what it can look like if one asserts autonomy by testing independence and interdependence as inextricable, empowering forces. . . . Living in Hauser's essay universe is comfortable and encouraging for anyone who relishes the untamed, wild places."

—TRINIE DALTON, author of *Wide Eyed* and *Baby Geisha*

"Hauser's book is and isn't about being a member of the Disney family. What it *is* about is gender identity, privilege, cultural appropriation, and how these do and don't meld together. This is a wild, stunning, unfiltered, and stylistically groundbreaking memoir—a fascinating juxtaposition between what is and isn't real. It will blow your Mickey Mouse ears off."

—SUE WILLIAM SILVERMAN, author of *How to Survive Death and Other Inconveniences*

It's fun to be a person I don't know

American Lives   SERIES EDITOR: TOBIAS WOLFF

It's fun to be a person I don't know

CHACHI D. HAUSER

UNIVERSITY OF NEBRASKA PRESS   *Lincoln*

The University of Nebraska Press is part of a land-grant institution with campuses and programs on the past, present, and future homelands of the Pawnee, Ponca, Otoe-Missouria, Omaha, Dakota, Lakota, Kaw, Cheyenne, and Arapaho Peoples, as well as those of the relocated Ho-Chunk, Sac and Fox, and Iowa Peoples.

Set and designed in Questa by N. Putens.

Library of Congress Cataloging-in-Publication Data
Names: Hauser, Chachi D., author.
Title: It's fun to be a person I don't know / Chachi D. Hauser.
Description: Lincoln: University of Nebraska Press, [2023] | Series: American lives | Includes bibliographical references.
Identifiers: LCCN 2022026638
ISBN 9781496233158 (paperback)
ISBN 9781496235602 (epub)
ISBN 9781496235619 (pdf)
Subjects: LCSH: Hauser, Chachi D. | Disney family. | Walt Disney Company. | Women authors, American—Biography. | Women motion picture producers and directors—United States—Biography. | BISAC: BIOGRAPHY & AUTOBIOGRAPHY / Personal Memoirs | SOCIAL SCIENCE / Gender Studies
Classification: LCC PS3608.A87613 A3 2023 | DDC 325.9—dc24/eng/20221205
LC record available at https://lccn.loc.gov/2022026638

For Nonna

contents

author's note   ix

this summer, high river   1

the boys who wouldn't grow up   9

steamboat   29

ashes   39

grand isle part I   56

disneyfication   64

grand isle part II   90

imagineering   102

delta dawn   121

road trip   139

we should kiss between our sigh   158

acknowledgments   179

notes   181

author's note

Though this book is based on things I actually lived, I've tried to arrange these experiences into a narrative. Like a documentary film, this book is a construction; if everything I've ever experienced is the footage, a lot has fallen to the cutting room floor. I have made myself, as well as my family, friends, and lovers into characters. For this reason, nearly all the names have been changed.

It's fun to be a person I don't know

this summer, high river

Our bed smells of his sweat. At night my skin absorbs his skin whether or not he's beside me. My body smells like his now—I've forgotten my own smell. For months on end, the River has pulsed swollen beside our city, New Orleans—record amounts of rain and melted winter snows up North moving toward the Gulf through the deep path called the Mississippi, carved in the earth by water and reinforced by humans. Now, its need for release threatens our false peace. Upstream, the River has already flooded millions of acres of farmland. I almost feel sorry for the River. I almost want to free it myself, if only my hands were strong enough to peel apart the levees on either side of the brown water like a pair of thighs. Each day we wake, we drive over potholed pavement, streets like choppy sea, move in and out of buildings I'm not sure will hold. As the rain falls, we watch anxiously through distorted glass as water gathers around tires, as it creeps up the bodies of our cars with so much want.

*

On the plaster walls of a community center in Mississippi, in the early 1950s, Walter Anderson painted murals. In 2019 I stand beside P—his lean body towering a foot above mine, his back slightly stooped over, as always, so he can hear me—in front of one of Anderson's scenes: pelicans

made up of pastel patches of sunlight and blue clouds, wings expanding
across sky. Often, artist and naturalist Anderson rowed himself eight
miles out to Horn Island, a skinny barrier island, to be completely alone
for weeks on end. There, he painted and wrote about the creatures he
observed. Once, when the dark clouds of Betsy came rolling over the Gulf,
he tied his boat and his body to the trunk of a tree. P and I walk through
the small, quiet Walter Anderson museum in Ocean Springs with sinking bellies full of fried cheese bombs. On our drive back to New Orleans
from Dauphin Island, we'd made a pit stop to see P's childhood friend
at the restaurant where he now works, Woody's, a counterfeit Apple-
bee's on a main street of hot, moving metal and strip malls. Across the
bay the massive casinos of Biloxi jut out on the edge of the Mississippi
Sound, flaunting their impossibility, their excess. Anderson wished to
preserve the natural landscape of the Gulf Coast, to convince others of
the urgency of his desire—with his paintings, hoping to show that the
swampy landscape, the brown-water beaches, had more to offer us than
oil. I walk through these muted, over-air-conditioned rooms, walls filled
with his paintings, streaks of greens, blues, purples—a tree, a crab, an
alligator—and keep thinking this museum feels like a celebration of
his failure.

*

There's a girl P wants to have sex with again, and he says he wants me
to be there, to be a part of it somehow. He's able to put this into words
only in her presence, though, and not in mine. I see their bare feet swinging over the bayou's green surface, their hands resting on hot cement,
propping up their torsos as they sit next to each other, the space between
their bodies more purposeful than an embrace. *Would you want to sleep
over at our house sometime?* he asks, again making me into a phantom
limb with which he can reach out and touch her. She laughs girlishly,
eyes closing to a squint, strands of her brown bangs falling into them,
surprised by his forwardness. She says she'll think about it.

*

As I write this, the streets are filling again with water. As I write this, I'm easily distracted and have a bad taste in my mouth and can't stop picking at the skin on the edges of my face. I used to find meaning in so many meaningless things. I used to get angrier. How many words will I write in my lifetime and how many more will I destroy before they even meet the page? How many words will it take to unearth myself, whoever I am inside this body? The rain keeps falling.

*

Walter Anderson wrote in one of his journals: "Nature does not like to be anticipated . . . but loves to surprise; in fact seems to justify itself to man in that way, restoring his youth to him each time—the true fountain of youth."[1] Betsy was the same one that leveled my great-grandparents' house in Bay St. Louis in 1965, sparing only a porcelain toilet, a bottle of whiskey hidden in its tank—when they surveyed the wreckage, both of my great-grandparents denied being the one to put it there. They went to Los Angeles to stay with my mom's family and never moved back to the Gulf Coast. Instead, in 2013, I did. In 2005 many of Anderson's writings and paintings were damaged when Hurricane Katrina destroyed his former home in Ocean Springs, still inhabited at the time by one of his children. Each time I think of red wine spilled on yellow sheets, the skin that smells like mine moving against skin that doesn't, I am made younger, younger still. I imagine his tongue pressing into her. I am a child, lowering myself into the hot water of a bath, still surprised by how a feeling can contain both a sting and a caress.

*

My friends rent a stilted house on Dauphin Island for the second summer in a row and, this time, P comes with me. Last year the trip was only a week after he fucked her, when he finally forced our open relationship into the realm of the real, a space I was no longer sure I wanted to inhabit. We were still pretending to be broken up, so I went without him. I had just cut off all my hair again, shaved my head to skin and stubble. One night I took a molly-like drug my friend couldn't remember the name of,

placed its bitter powder under my tongue, and soon sensed the presence
of my short-haired, twelve-year-old self sitting beside me. I am still them,
I realized—a genderless child. While my friends curled up on sandy
couches watching Seinfeld, I danced alone down a skinny beach on the
bay side, running to the very edge of the island, trying to find the edge of
myself, and swore the dark water was dancing with me. This summer I
bring P to the same beach at night, and we walk down a long, thin pier,
uneven like an old roller coaster track, like the Coney Island Cyclone,
stretching out into the Mississippi Sound. We have sex at the end of its
reach, my back on the hard slatted-wood surface, fish jumping beneath
us, their bodies slapping water again and again.

*

For years, I have been unable to write a sentence that surprises me. I
never thought I'd find these words amongst the wreckage. How could a
part of myself get lost and then find its way back? I'm a New York City
kid, finally finding dirt underneath all that concrete.

*

P sends her pictures of his skin and also pictures of maps: the storm's
potential path toward the Gulf Coast. I'm not proud of why I know this,
the text messages living on his computer left open in our bedroom. I
scroll through the story of all I don't know, unable to stop myself. In
these messages, P speaks in a voice I haven't heard in five years, a voice
full of want, a voice that seems to know of its own foolishness yet still
flows forward uncontrollably from his fingers, an un-leveed River moving toward an end it doesn't know. It's been exactly a year since they
fucked, but he asks her if she wants to drive down from Baton Rouge to
New Orleans to spend the hurricane with us. I am surprised again by
my jealousy. I don't want him to speak to me that way. Instead, I want
to be the one who can speak like this. I want to inherit his confidence,
his ability to make a person undone.

*

After we have sex on the pier, I lower myself, still naked, down a wooden ladder into the water. P refuses to join me. He says the bay is gross in the light of day—brown water and toxic runoff from the Mississippi River, the Gulf's "dead zone," made stagnant in this inlet between island and coast—but I don't care. We are so far out from the shore and yet it's still shallow, only up to my shins, so I drop to my knees and fall forward, submerging my torso. I pull myself through the water like an alligator, curling my fingers into muddy sand. I crawl further and further out, toward the small burning lights of oil rigs, but the bottom never drops; it never gets any deeper. I spread my arms; I push water on either side to propel myself a little faster. Then I notice: each stroke lights up tiny jellyfish like fireflies. They don't sting me; instead, their veins briefly fill with glow at my touch. I know they do not think, they do not feel, the way we do. Still, are they surprised by their own light?

*

We lounge on blankets in scratchy grass at night, watching a movie projected on a big screen in my friends' backyard. I rest my skull on P's thigh. Sweat pools under the tightness of my sports bra, and my legs are slippery, perspiration mingling with bug spray—the familiar amalgamation of scents we gather in summertime. I like how, when I lie on my back, my breasts spread to the sides of my chest, flattening, becoming less obvious. Sometimes, when I'm naked in bed, I tug each breast toward an armpit, tucking the skin and tissue beneath each arm. I admire my flat chest. Once, I showed P my trick and he laughed. I laughed too, but I wasn't sure what I was laughing at. He told me he liked my breasts. The train moans louder than the screams of a woman in the horror film we're watching, and I remember where I am: at the edge of this tattered country, in a city that feels somehow both exposed and cradled. Here, we sink into the earth, melt into the earth like sleep, forgetting we live on an island. When will we wake up from this dream?

*

There used to be no public access to the Mississippi River in New Orleans. It was an active port, so the banks of the River were stacked with docks and warehouses, water hidden from view by these large structures and high floodwalls. Near Jackson Square, beside the famous green-and-white-striped awning of Café Du Monde, tourists stood on a teetering ladder, propped against the concrete flood barrier, to get a glimpse of the River, to take photographs of its brown surface.[2] Mayor "Moon" Landrieu said the sight of these tourists was the reason he dedicated himself to building the promenade along the River dubbed the "Moon Walk," completed in the '70s and accessible from the French Quarter—he wanted to satisfy their desperate need to see the River, which drove them up ladders, scaling walls designed to keep the water out.

*

On the bank of the Mississippi River I push J's long hair out of his face, behind his ear. I hold his jaw in my palm like a piece of fruit. It's almost morning but it's still dark. We've been walking around the Bywater all night—from bar to bar—and, without much deliberation, found ourselves moving toward the Mississippi, as if drawn by a magnet. Downriver from the Moon Walk, in the Bywater, a park runs along the River—the park closes after sunset, made inaccessible by a very tall chain-link fence and gates, padlocked around dusk. J and I are banged up from scaling the fence, from falling down onto cement, just so we could come watch the dark River, just so we could be completely alone, even if for only a few hours. When we get to the water's edge, we let the rocks draw us down onto them to bruise ourselves further. He moves his hands over my chest, flattened by a binder, and I am surprised by my confidence. I'm surprised by how easy it is to pull these new hips, even though I feel the weight of his body and recognize it is unfamiliar.

*

I don't know why we do this to each other, but it seems necessary, to keep hurting, to keep finding new ways to hurt.

*

The night before the hurricane is supposed to really hit, P and I walk through the Quarter to see how high the River is. Strong, circling winds swirl trash around the sidewalks of Bourbon Street while clouds are pushed quickly past the almost-full moon. The River has been record high for months, above flood stage for most of the year, so everyone is worried this storm will be the one to really screw us. The River is projected to topple the levees. Still, P and I have decided to stay in New Orleans and, for some reason, tonight it feels appropriate to go look at the very thing that might destroy us. We walk through Jackson Square to the entrance of the Moon Walk and find the colossal floodwalls barricaded, an alarm perpetually sounding, the River inaccessible—we've never seen it like this before. Having walked all the way over here, we decide to get beignets at Café Du Monde, the usually overcrowded outdoor seating nearly empty, just a few confused tourists trying to salvage their vacations. Above us, the green-and-white-striped awning thrashes about in the wind while P and I sit with powdered sugar in our laps. I ask him if he thinks the storm will be as bad as they say, knowing he does not have an answer.

*

I've had sex with so many women like that, J says. I look over at the pretty, short-haired girl with lipstick, hoop earrings, a tube top, leather boots with heels. We are standing outside a bar in the Bywater around two in the morning. We haven't walked to the River yet—we will soon—but for now we are still just two new friends, alone together for the first time, with the option of remaining platonic. *I've never known how to be a woman like that,* I respond, watching the pretty girl gesture wildly to her friend, her smiling mouth full of gossip, a cigarette between manicured fingers. *Well, I'm not sure I've ever known how to be a woman,* I concede. *That's what I like about you,* J tells me matter-of-factly, *you're not a woman, you're more malleable than that.* His word choice moves through me haltingly, *malleable*—like something he wants to mold with his hands, a thought I both like and don't. *Malleable*—like a river that could be contained, convinced, by an infrastructure of his making. At the same time, I know in this moment that it will happen, that we will find ourselves pressing against each other somewhere, because I am surprised he can see this, when P cannot. *Fluid*, I think, I wish he'd said *fluid*.

*

P asks her to spend the hurricane with us, but she doesn't. She stays in Baton Rouge, where the storm is supposed to be less severe. For a weekend that seems to last years, P and I stay inside, checking nervously out the window as dark clouds move above us, but it hardly even rains. When the radio tells us it's okay to go outside again, we are confused and don't know how to adjust back to normal life. The storm does not come; the River does not topple the levees. Still we are here. Still we wait.

*

The day after finding myself with J at the riverbank, a few weeks after the storm did not come, I'm hungover and exhausted from having barely slept; I'd climbed into bed with P around 6:00 a.m. and talked to him about what happened until there were no more words. In the afternoon P is sleeping, and I walk a few blocks to get myself a coffee, to force myself to eat food, to try to feel like I'm still here. I sit in a loud, busy coffee shop, sipping an espresso that doesn't taste right, because nothing does, and keep finding new bruises. It starts to rain, hard, but I need to go home, I need to lie down again, so I walk through the downpour back to our apartment. On our street the water is already up to the curb, inching up faster, lapping at my ankles as I run through the alleyway, up the metal stairs, pulling myself toward our second-floor apartment, toward P sleeping on the couch. The water keeps chasing me.

the boys who wouldn't grow up

The walkway moves slowly, but I still fear that moment when my small hand must relinquish its hold on the railing. My feet step off of steady ground onto the uncertain surface, which indifferently transports my six-year-old body forward like a suitcase at an airport baggage claim. Moving alongside the conveyor belt under neon green lights are small pirate ships of different colors with billowing plastic sails. The twinkling instrumental soundtrack continues, and I hear the words in my head, *You can fly! You can fly!*

My father and I board one of the ships. He pulls the metal bar down to our laps, and our boat sails out of the waiting area into Wendy's lamp-lit bedroom. Wendy sits alone on her bed, as in the animated film—I've seen it so many times I know it by heart—when her father has just told her she can no longer sleep in the nursery with her younger brothers. She can't tell her stories anymore; she has to grow up. We hear Peter's voice, *Off to Neverland!*, but don't see him. The boat is weightless, soaring up over the scene, out of Wendy's pink bedroom and over the glowing city of London. The city gets smaller and smaller beneath us.

We move into a new, distinct space: the vibrant Neverland. The world is dark, an endless nighttime, but the steep green island hills are phosphorescent. We fly over a pirate ship, small down below us, and over a group of mermaids lounging on rocks. We fly over Tiger Lily and a circle of "Indians" beating robotically on drums—I do not yet understand the violence contained by these caricatures, but I notice my dad shuddering at the sight of them.

We sail past a large pirate ship and a scene of combat: life-sized robots Peter and Captain Hook are balanced on a yard of the ship's mast, sword-fighting. Meanwhile, Wendy teeters at the edge of the plank, so vulnerable in only her nightgown. Pirates stand on the deck, leering menacingly at her. They've tied her younger brothers to the mast. There is something about this ride that never fails to make my young stomach churn. Maybe it's seeing all those kids in such real danger with no adults to help them. Maybe it's the darkness or the sensation of being suspended in air, above the action, with no escape. Maybe it's because, though I'm scared, a part of me still wants to be Peter, sword-fighting—how much I'd rather be him than the defenseless Wendy.

Soon, Peter is at the helm of the ship, Wendy is free, and pirates are strewn across the deck, defeated, dead. In the water beside the boat, Hook is balanced precariously between the jaws of a crocodile.

The ride is brief, but the completeness of its narrative is satisfying. Our boat flies slowly back into the waiting area. My eyes adjust to the bright light as my dad and I hop back out onto the moving walkway and make our way to the exit.

*

When I went on the Peter Pan ride in Disney World more recently, in my late twenties, the ellipses in time—how quickly they occur as the ride-goer is transported through space—reminded me of film editing. The ride uses the separate, contained space of each room to move the ride-goer into a new setting, a new line of action. The walls between these rooms exist as cuts, collapsing the time between scenes into a quick blink.

*

When I am nine or ten, my mom tells me how, in theatrical renditions of Peter Pan, the titular character is traditionally played by a woman with short hair. I'm surprised and want so badly to see this for myself. I secretly hope my mom will take me to such a production someday. This seems oddly subversive for a story I've always closely associated with Disney, even though it's not originally a Disney story (and even though Peter is voiced by a little boy in the animated film, and in the parks, the character is played awkwardly by a male cast member in his twenties). In a culture so obsessed with the alleged rules of gender, why is this one exception made for the sake of theatrical truth? The casting choice is, to me, an admission: a girl can be a boy, perhaps more convincingly than an actual boy can.

In hearing about the custom of a woman playing the part of the perpetual boy, I feel the tug of something familiar. When my mom first tells me this, I have short hair and wear baggy T-shirts and baseball hats. I am often mistaken for a boy. What if this skill—to disguise my gender, to become a little boy—somehow overlapped with the ability to fly?

*

A few years ago, I flew from New Orleans to Mexico City to visit my sister for a long weekend and ended up getting drinks with Matthew, a guy I'd been obsessed with in college but now considered myself to be over. My sister was sharing an apartment in Juárez, near Zona Rosa, for a few months with another ex-pat, a guy from Germany. She'd made a few friends there, other queer people and artists, both Mexicans and transplants. I'd been to Mexico City once before, when I was six and my sister was five. There is a photo of us two in a park filled with lush vegetation, posing proudly in recently purchased outfits, my sister wearing a purple dress and cowboy boots and me in a Mexican soccer uniform. Now, I was startled to have found myself in an area of Mexico City not unlike recent incarnations of Bed-Stuy or the Bywater—McDonald's and family-owned bodegas alongside hip, sterile coffee shops and warmly lit restaurants filled with young, tattooed patrons—neighborhoods altered to appeal to people like me. Still Mexico, with taco meat grilling on every corner and carts of fresh fruit, yet gentrification there had taken a familiar form. Newly painted murals of Frida Kahlo and colorfully dressed skeletons adorned walls of blighted buildings, pleading obnoxiously to be contained by the small frame of an Instagram post.

I arrived Thursday evening and went with my sister and her friends to a clown-themed drag show that lasted until morning. We laughed ourselves silly watching a queen making a balloon animal that she proceeded to sensually deep-throat. On Friday, after waking up groggily, I emailed Matthew to meet up that night. I wouldn't have known he was in Mexico, but my sister had run into him a few days earlier in front of a neighborhood taco cart—his unmistakable lanky, long-armed gait, her curly hair lit by fluorescent light as she stuffed a taco in her lipsticked mouth. Last I knew, he was in LA or Chicago, editing a documentary he'd been working on since the brief period when we dated seven years earlier. At the time I thought of our breakup as a mutual agreement, though I spent the following years thinking of him constantly and asking myself why, if we'd parted amicably, we never spoke.

While we were together, a guy in Matthew's grade confided to me drunkenly one night he was certain Matthew was an "actual genius"; I would hear others describe Matthew this way after he'd graduated. Two years after we broke up, during my senior year of college, I won a school writing prize for an essay I wrote about Matthew, a story far more romantic than the reality. The essay was about how the roles of artist and muse are not mutually exclusive because, in watching him write and direct a short film, I'd been inspired to make art of my own.

I experienced love for Matthew as a bodily anxiety I couldn't turn off, my hands shaking, my eyes rolling at every word that exited my stupid mouth. I was infatuated from the moment I first saw him on a film set in college, because he was older than me, because he seemed to have a strange brain and remarkable aloofness I wished to possess. I wanted him to respect me. I wanted his "genius" to infect me. I couldn't understand why this shy man was so much braver than I was; his silences seemed to speak so much more poignantly than mine.

Now, somehow, we were both in Mexico City and were meeting up to get drinks.

*

Alex and I are eleven years old and are both tomboys in oversized T-shirts and basketball shorts. Alex cuts her hair short in second grade, and I copy her because I am so drawn to her, her fearlessness and her swagger. Alex is always willing to put her body at risk for a stunt. She pummels into other players on the basketball court. She dives headfirst and does flips into the swimming pool in her mom's apartment building. She's always bounding around spaces with swiftness and confidence.

I imitate her. I want to walk like a boy like she does, so I watch her. She inhabits maleness so naturally, and I'm jealous of this. When a babysitter brings a group of us to Pizzeria Uno on 86th Street, Alex and I sneak away, disappear into the men's bathroom together, and emerge with laughter when we aren't identified as imposters. At some point, Alex tells me she's rigged up some kind of mechanism that allows her to pee standing up. She never shows me the device, so I'm always puzzled about how it really works, though I remain very curious, impressed by her inventiveness, her attempt to circumvent the obstacles of our gender.

We aren't permitted to wear pants at the Catholic all-girls school we go to, and I see how much it pains Alex to remove her sweatpants from beneath the mandatory plaid uniform skirt after being scolded by a teacher. I too feel naked with just a small piece of fabric hanging precariously over the tops of my thighs—a gust of wind or an enthusiastic movement is all that's required to expose us, to remind us of the embarrassment of our bodies and how these bodies are seen. We start wearing our gym shorts underneath our skirts.

I never understand the adult need to police Alex's clothing choices—at our Catholic school, the disapproval is marked by feelings of sinfulness, of guilt, because we are indoctrinated, both of us altar girls (although neither of my parents are believers)—but this need permeates every aspect of her life. Alex is adopted, and her adoptive parents are in their sixties and divorced and seem, even to me as a child, very unhappy. Her father remarried an awful, prissy woman who forces Alex to wear dresses and to go to a therapist to examine why, exactly, she hates wearing dresses so much. Because of the divorce court ruling, though, Alex spends more time at her mother's place, an apartment in a brutal-looking thirty-eight-floor red brick building on 89th and Madison. Alex prefers this arrangement because, for the most part, her mom lets her wear what she wants. Her mother is retired and is always locked up in her bedroom alone, smoking cigarettes and consuming bottles of liquor as daytime legal dramas drone on meaninglessly, unseen behind the closed doors. She seldom comes out to check on us. I always return from sleepovers there with the stench of smoke in my clothes and having eaten only pizza Bagel Bites or Hot Pockets for dinner.

At Alex's mom's apartment we can swear. We imitate the characters on South Park. We say "fuck" every chance we get. We play Tony Hawk's Pro Skater, which lets us shape-shift into actual men who skillfully maneuver skateboards on half-pipes and move through abandoned buildings and other places we'd never be allowed to go, places we wouldn't even know how to find in our overly inhabited city. At Alex's place we play basketball in the hallway with her neighbor, a boy around our age. Since we go to an all-girls school, we try to soak up any male influence we're exposed to. We dunk on her neighbor's tiny plastic hoop, made for children smaller than us, pushing each other and running eagerly through the confined spaces of our carpeted-hallway playground.

*

Maybe it's a myth, but someone once told me Peter Pan was usually played by a woman for the practical reason that women are lighter, making hoisting them up on harnesses for flying tricks easier.

In 1904 the Broadway producer of the first stage production of *Peter Pan*, Charles Frohman, was apparently the first to suggest a young woman be cast as the lead. Frohman, reasoning it would be misguided to cast a grown man for the role and that casting a boy would require the other children to be scaled down in age accordingly, asked if his female protégé, Maude Adams, could play the role in the American production.[1] Frohman also advised J. M. Barrie to rename the play after its main character instead of using his working title, "The Great White Father," which is what the Native American characters call Peter in the play. From its inception the play was inseparable from its narrative of colonialism, Peter Pan as the white savior, and its caricature of Native Americans.[2] The animated Disney version unabashedly celebrates and even furthers Barrie's hateful depictions—so many children have grown up watching those animated stereotypes beating their drums, singing the original Disney song "What Made the Red Man Red?" Contemporary productions struggle with the fact that Neverland's tribe of Native Americans is impossible to expunge from the story or to represent in a manner that's not offensive. Barrie's story still gets retold though, over and over again, as if there are no new stories, as we pretend there's nothing nefarious in perpetuating these ideas.

In the first film version of Barrie's play, a silent feature made in 1924, Peter Pan was played by Betty Bronson, a seventeen-year-old girl. Wanting an unknown to originate this part for the screen, Barrie handpicked Bronson for her first big role. She wore her curly hair cut short for the part. Curls tucked under a pointed cap and her delicate, boyish features, along with her ballerina-like grace, captivated the moviegoing public.

"I want always to be a little boy and have fun," Peter Pan exclaims to Wendy and her mother, Mrs. Darling, in one of the 1924 film's final intertitles. After refusing Mrs. Darling's offer to adopt him, Peter pleads for Wendy to leave with him, back to Neverland. Wendy almost caves, putting her head to Peter's chest and saying, "But he does so need a mother," feeling for the last time the seductive call of her complicated position as both love interest and mother to Peter. Wendy's mother refuses to let her go with him; however, Mrs. Darling promises Wendy can go visit Peter for one week of every year to do his "spring cleaning."

In this moment Peter and Wendy's relationship becomes one defined by its silences, by long periods of absence, and it's inevitable they will grow apart since only one of them is growing.

Standing in the window, Wendy and Mrs. Darling both tenderly kiss Peter, or Betty, goodbye.

*

Matthew and I met up in front of a dark, bougie "shamanism-themed" bar in Mexico City someone had recommended to Matthew but, he assured me upon entering it, he'd never been to before. The bartender was carefully concocting a beverage that was spitting out large plumes of smoke or steam. We laughed at this show and found a table tucked in a corner. Sipping on mezcal Matthew told me how a production company we'd both worked for as interns was now producing the documentary he was directing—he was living in Mexico City for a few months to work with an editor here on it. He'd been shooting for many years and, over that time, he'd apparently been rejected by every grant he'd applied for except one, yet he seemed unshaken—the film would be made, and seen, and I believed him. Since college, I'd become suspicious about the several boys I knew who were deemed "geniuses" by their peers, yet I still knew Matthew would make his film happen, somehow, and that it would be well received. I told him about a short film I'd spent the past year making in New Orleans and how disappointing it was to continuously receive festival rejections. I told him about how each rejection email thrust me into a new crisis, each one admittedly milder than the last, but nonetheless making me feel more and more that directing was not something I was chalked up to do: *Who was I to make films anyway?* He did not share this preoccupation, and he was very encouraging about my films. I appreciated his reassurance while also hating him for it. I wanted so badly to be an artist like him, to be confident in my work like him. He made it look so easy.

*

Late at night, long after Alex's mother passes out, Alex and I stare at the desktop computer in the living room. We wait anxiously as the dial-up screeches away to cherish the anonymity of AOL chatrooms. I don't get how Alex knows how to talk to people in those chatrooms. Alex always sits in the office chair and I stand behind her, gripping the back of the chair and watching her type. I see the sentences appear on the large, glowing screen and hope she won't ask me to switch places with her, because I would not know how to speak to those strangers the way she does.

Alex tells the aliases contained in little boxes that she's an older girl, like fifteen. She asks them what they want her to do to them. She tells them she's taking off her clothes, narrating each removal in her fictional striptease, always culminating with "panties," a word that makes me cringe. She tells them she's doing what they want her to do, which involves "B.J.s" and "H.J.s" and "sucking dick" and "being wet," all of which I only half understand.

Do these faceless strangers know they're talking to two children, two boy-girls for whom the chatroom is another video game? Maybe, occasionally, they're children on the other end too. The words Alex is saying and those strangers are saying seem so detached from our actual bodies and what we can do with them. I wonder how Alex learned to perform both boyness and girlness so adeptly. I also fear that, if what Alex says over the internet is girlness, I will never really be a girl myself.

*

After the 1924 film *Peter Pan*, Betty Bronson went on to have a few more big roles, playing wholesome teenagers in the silent films *Are Parents People?* and *A Kiss for Cinderella*.[3] In 1925 she played the Virgin Mary in *Ben Hur: A Tale of the Christ*, the most expensive silent film ever made. Her career, however, dissipated as popular tastes changed in the late '20s—Bronson's character-type of the innocent virgin was replaced by the rowdy, short-skirted flapper, and Paramount's attempt to reinvent Bronson as such was ultimately a failure.

Betty Bronson retired from the screen in 1933. After playing Peter, the eternal boy, she couldn't be received by the public as a sexualized female character.

*

Like Peter, growing up means I can't be a little boy anymore. At twelve my body begins to deny the story told by my clothing. As breasts start to form beneath my Yankees T-shirts, people no longer mistake me for male. To make matters worse, Alex, my partner in crime, moves to another city, and we quickly fall out of touch. So soon I will become an object of desire—boys will start to notice me, signaling their approval through comments that make my stomach turn and touches I will be disturbed to find make me feel nothing at all—but, first, there's a transitional phase: I learn to be ashamed of my misgendered moment and thus start growing out my hair and ask my mom to let me pierce my ears. My hair takes a painfully long time to grow. For a few years I wear a bandana, folded into a triangle and tied at the nape of my neck, like a bandage, covering my unsightly hair as it moves through all its awkward phases.

*

In college I made my first short film about the period in my life when I was twelve and the shame took form. In the movie, a young girl with short hair, Lolo, goes on a field trip with her class to a planetarium. There, she's told by a woman in the bathroom that she's made a mistake, *the boys' room is around the corner*. Lolo, embarrassed, not sure what to do, obligingly goes to the men's room. When she emerges her teacher sees her and reprimands her for using the incorrect bathroom. After this, Lolo starts to wear a bandana around her hair and no longer wears sweatpants beneath her uniform skirts. Ultimately, she finds a friend: another girl at school who is reprimanded by the same teacher for wearing basketball sneakers instead of the uniform-mandated dress shoes. In the final scene, Lolo cuts this girl's hair in the locker room—long brown hair falls to the floor. They smile at each other in the large mirror.

The bathroom incident in the film is loosely based on something that happened at an airport when I was twelve. Waiting for our plane to board, I left my family sitting with our bags and entered the women's bathroom alone. An older woman took it upon herself to direct me to the *correct* bathroom, the men's bathroom, which was at the other end of the corridor. I was scared of telling the woman she'd made a mistake—in a way, I wasn't sure she had—so I went, for the first time without Alex, into the cavernous yellow-lit men's room. I averted my eyes from the big men standing at urinals, hoping I wouldn't be found out. I locked myself in a stall, wishing to never have to emerge again. It was deeply unsettling to be a young person teetering on the border between genders and to be instructed by external sources on where I belonged. I didn't like being told which bathroom to use, instead of choosing for myself, as I had with Alex. Afterward, I walked back to where my parents were sitting, thinking they could see the shame on my face, but they didn't notice. In this version, the real-life version, I did not find a friend at my school and cut her hair—Alex was gone, I was alone. Instead, I grew my hair long.

*

At some point, in a different bar we'd roamed to, called Scary Bar and themed accordingly, Matthew began to apologize for having been a shitty boyfriend. Though he wasn't very specific in his apologies, I cried a little—I'd wanted to hear this for some time but didn't think it would ever happen. Matthew always had trouble expressing his feelings. During the eight months we'd dated, we said we loved each other only once—a few weeks after he graduated, on the last night we spent together before he moved away from the East Coast to Chicago. I was very drunk and was the first to say it. Thankfully, he reciprocated, but we never said it again.

Without really addressing it, we started walking back toward his place to have a few more beers. Every time I'd ever slept with Matthew, even when we were dating, it had been due to my strong-willed pursuit, so I didn't think much of the implication of the situation: sitting on his bed in his one-room studio because of a lack of real furniture. I didn't know he would adopt an intimate position, lying on his belly next to me, his shoulder touching mine, or tell me that I could stay the night if I wanted, but he did. I pressed him on this point, perhaps because I needed him to really say it. He told me I wouldn't have to sleep on the floor if that's what I was asking. *But what do you really mean, stay over?* I had to ask him a few times before he told me that he would kiss me and I would stay over and that's what he meant. He asked me if I thought P would care, a tactless question, and I momentarily allowed myself to ask it too.

I had to leave. It was four in the morning, and I had to get out of there. I held my face in my hands. I closed my eyes because I was scared if I looked at him for long enough it would happen and it would be terrible, especially if I liked it, and I was pretty sure I would. Needing so much to be respected by him, I could confuse desire and respect, and I knew I would make myself completely available to him if he just tried. Matthew walked me downstairs to get a cab. It was drizzling and we hugged in the street, but he didn't want to commit to the embrace—I had to pull his body close. I got into the car, and I sat there on the leather seat like I'd won the interaction, but then, as the car lurched away, I started to weep. When would I see him again, and in what context? If we saw each other at a film festival, would he pretend we were merely professional peers—would he act like this never happened? In a way, I already knew he would. How I wanted to feel secure in my artistic pursuits, as he always seemed to. How I wanted to nonchalantly wander back into his life, to ask him to sleep over like it was nothing. How I wanted to be

Peter. The rain obscured the window, and the usually crowded city was empty and wet and quiet.

*

When I'm in fourth grade, my class puts on a production of *Peter Pan*. Peter is played by a girl—at our all-girls school, all the parts are, of course. Lena, a teacher's pet and, I've recently decided, my nemesis, is Peter. I watch Lena, a ponytail of smooth brown hair tucked into her pointed green cap, with her hands proudly resting on her hips in Peter's classic pose.

Always a very shy kid, I'm usually cast in bit parts, my teachers kindly limiting my opportunities for public speaking. My biggest role was as Mary in our third grade nativity play. The role was big in name only, as I had a single line and spent most of my stage time posed in my blue cloak in the same seated position, cradling a bunched-up towel, gazing upon it with the unmatched adoration of a virgin who's just birthed the son of god.

In our production of *Peter Pan*, I'm cast as one of the lost boys and have two lines, one of them spoken and one of them in a song. Alex is a lost boy too, and we are the only ones in the play without ponytails stuffed into our caps—we really look the part. I wear a backward baseball cap and hate every moment of being on stage, being looked at and scrutinized by the audience, made up of parents and kids in other grades. My spoken line goes okay, as it's only a few words, but when the moment comes for my singing line, my mind goes completely blank. I hear our teacher plinking away at the piano, the notes progressing in the way that signals I should be singing, but I'm not. My stomach twists and I know it's too late—how could I be so scared of my own voice? How could I miss my line in front of all these people? Afterward, my classmates tease me, but it's nothing compared to the harsh words I speak to myself for being so cowardly. I don't like being looked at, because I don't know what others see when they see me—I didn't realize, until this moment, this fear was capable of growing so strong I would be made silent, as if I could make my body disappear if I only followed my voice to whatever dark corner it had escaped to.

*

Sometimes—often, really—I'm still the little lost boy, missing my line in front of all those expectant faces. When asked about my opinions on art, my filmmaking work, my writing, I get so scared, despite how confident I feel when I'm alone, writing. Public speaking continues to seem impossible for me, even though I've had to do it more and more. For some reason I can never come up with the words to explain myself *aloud*.

*

In the 1924 silent film, Peter (Betty Bronson) and Wendy (played by Mary Brian) first meet in Wendy's bedroom, Peter entering through the window as she sleeps. That night Wendy sews Peter's disconnected shadow back on. As Wendy carefully sews the shadow to his toes, Peter winces in pain. When the shadow is secured, Peter dances around the room, watching his shadow obediently follow his movements. "Cock-a-doodle-doo!" reads an intertitle as Peter lauds his own cleverness, arms outstretched. Watching his celebration, Wendy looks distraught and tells Peter if she's no use, she'll just withdraw. She gets back into bed, pulling the blanket over her face. "I can't help crowing, Wendy, when I am pleased with myself," Peter says. He sits on the footboard of her bed and playfully kicks her. Then he concedes, "Wendy, one girl is more use than twenty boys." This pleases Wendy, and she gets out from under the covers. The two of them sit beside each other on the edge of her bed, and she tells Peter, flirtatiously, she will give him a kiss. Not sure what this means, Peter holds out his hand. Wendy, looking a little confused and disappointed, places a thimble into his palm. Peter jumps around the room, admiring the thimble. He gives Wendy an acorn, a "kiss" he calls it, in return.

*

From my teens into my early twenties—ever since my hair was long enough I felt I could remove the bandana—I wore my hair long, scared to cut it, ashamed of how I'd been seen in that airport bathroom. I wore red lipstick, copious amounts of black eyeliner, and form-fitting dresses, though almost always with Doc Martens. In high school I started piercing my face and, once, when I was still underage, retreated to the dirty backroom of a bong shop to get a shitty tattoo of a barcode—these aesthetic modifications I did only for myself, to take ownership of my body after it had been so heavily controlled for nine years of Catholic school. Otherwise, I tried to look like a typical girl. In photos I puffed my chest out, my breasts squeezed into a push-up bra, and sucked my cheeks in, yet inadvertently looked sheepishly away from the lens. When I walked I moved my hips sensually back and forth the way I thought a girl does. I smiled to myself when guys called out at me on the street. I liked when the popular guys in my high school noticed me, especially since I was one of the weird girls. I made out with these guys at parties and would pretend not to mind when they didn't acknowledge me in the hallway the following week. There was something powerful about tricking a preppy guy into finding me, a freak, attractive. At times the attention was a drug, even if what garnered it was a performance that strayed from my natural state. From high school into college, the need for the drug led me into the beds of so many stupid guys I had to stop counting, especially as this began to feel like an anthropological study I was conducting to see into strangers' bedrooms. (Alarmingly often, I was deriving far more joy from this "study" than from the sex.) One night, naked beside a boy I was hooking up with, I asked him if he would still like me if I shaved my head. When he replied with a resounding *no*, this idea became a sad inside joke of ours; I found myself always "threatening" him with my sheared scalp.

During my last month of college, having just finished my short film and inspired by my young self, I finally cut my hair again. I hacked the ponytail off and asked my friend to shave the rest. Now, I shave my head every month or so. I've stopped wearing dresses, unable to deny how much more comfortable I find a pair of jeans to be, how dresses make me feel naked. I find it funny how people I've known for a long time sometimes react to my shaved head and less feminine clothing, their discomfort made plain by their need to tell me I still look *pretty*. Seeing me, my mom tells me she would never cut her hair because she thinks my dad doesn't find short hair on women attractive.

Recently, I was alone at the New Orleans airport, waiting for my plane to board. It was early in the morning, before sunrise, and I was groggily washing my hands in a public bathroom when I heard a woman exclaim, *There's a dude in here!* Looking up from the sink, I saw no one else in the bathroom except for myself in the mirror, my baggy T-shirt and jeans, my shaved head. Looking at me longer, the woman quietly remarked, *Oh,* and carried on into a stall. As I walked out of the bathroom, I laughed to myself at the absurdity of it: the outrage in the woman's voice and yet how quickly she changed her tone. In my laughter there was also anger, not really at her, but at a world that was accepting of a girl pretending to be a boy only if she was hoisted up on ropes, only if it was make-believe. A world that was deeply confused by which bathroom someone who looked like me should use. I was glad to find, though, in my laughter there was no longer shame.

If it were the other way around—if I were a boy who looked like a girl, using the men's bathroom—I'm not sure the stranger could adjust so quickly to me after a closer look. I'm not sure his outrage would subside. In fact, the stranger's outrage would probably not appear until the reality of his "mistake" had set in; this is how people get killed, due to this exact type of rage. *Panic*, they call it, and juries understand how this could drive a man to murder. Masculinity is made up of its own structures of confinement, and I do not know what it is to live inside these walls, to try to find a way out.

                *

The day after Matthew's proposition was my last full day in Mexico City, and I wondered all day if we would see each other. My sister and I went to an expansive street market with some of her friends, and I got very sunburned and slightly buzzed off of Micheladas and bought a T-shirt with a glittering plastic applique, the name of a Mexican radio DJ on the front. That night, when it became clear I was really not going to see him, I couldn't control myself—I wrote him an email. Made weak again, forgetting all my professional resentments, I wrote of how the night before had confused me and how I sort of regretted my decision not to stay the night. I signed it with the word "love." Immediately after I'd sent it, the thought of the email made me recoil.

Two days later, after I'd left Mexico and gotten back home, he responded:

> Hope the rest of your trip was great. I'm not very good at expressing myself through emails or writing. Had such a great time on Saturday. I'm sure we'll be in the same city sometime sorta soon!
>
> Vid of a tightrope walker I saw yesterday . . .

Attached was a twenty-three-second video, shot from below, of a person on a tightrope, walking haltingly across the sky. I watched the video again and again, cherishing it like a kiss in the form of an acorn.

After seeing him in Mexico, I looked back, for the first time in years, at that essay I wrote in college and was bewildered by the wonder with which I'd described our relationship; I realized the narrative of my love for Matthew had completely shifted since then. I was embarrassed for my younger self, who loved Matthew so desperately they wrote a better relationship into being. Writing about Matthew was the only way I could have any ownership of him, the only way I could understand him. And, perhaps, the only way I could become more like him. I realized I was not writing a love story at all, despite what I thought at the time. I was writing about finding my own voice as an artist, searching the dark corners for wherever that voice was hiding.

I think what attracted me to him was something intangible, a fiction I continue to write and rewrite. The more he disappears, the more I want to create him, and in this way he has given me power. When I originally wrote about the concept of artist and muse and applied it to Matthew and me, I didn't realize that I needed to dismantle it even further—I needed to find the courage to become fully the artist, making him fully the muse.

*

Looking at an old picture of myself, my short hair and basketball jersey, I don't see a little girl. But I don't see a little boy either. I see a small body, a child's body, a kid who could move through space with confidence, a confidence I must've unlearned.

What I write has usually been defined—by others, not myself—as existing within the bounds of "creative nonfiction." This is because what I write emerges from my own experiences, my personal view of how events have occurred and how I process them. Between myself and the reader, there's an implicit understanding: I'm attempting to portray events as they happened, from my perspective. This genre gives me authority over the truth, at least my truth, and sometimes this scares me, maybe because my own truth seems murky even to me. Reading what I've written over the years, I remember how many different kinds of people I've been, how many voices I've adopted, created, inhabited. Toward the end of *Orlando*, her "biography" about a poet who changes from a man to a woman and lives over three hundred years, Virginia Woolf writes: "For [Orlando] had a great variety of selves to call upon, far more than we have been able to find room for, since a biography is considered complete if it accounts for six or seven selves, whereas a person may well have many thousand." This distinction, *nonfiction*, can feel incredibly limiting in its perimeters.

What I look like has usually been defined—by others, not myself—as existing within the bounds of "woman." Sometimes, I find myself holding my body in a manner that is uncomfortable but that I've adapted to in order to serve the definition of my gender. When I realize I'm doing this, for example when I've been sitting at length in public with my legs crossed or my knees pinned together, I have to remind myself to let the muscles loosen, to let my knees spread wide, leaning over to rest my elbows on my thighs, finding a different, more truthful, position.

The writer Robert Vivian talks about how *category* comes from the Greek *katēgoría*, meaning a public accusation. He says that to categorize a person or a piece of art is to speak against them. To confine oneself to the expectations of a genre, he posits, is to divide the self.[4]

*

In the last, dark room of the Disney ride, Peter stands with pride at the helm of the pirate ship, and Wendy stands beside him, a step below him, her hands calmly clasped as if in prayer. Her blue nightgown glows. I see it fluttering in the wind, but perhaps this is my imagination. Peter is smiling, his hands firmly planted on the ship's wheel, as it moves ever so slightly in his grasp. Wendy's animatronic head moves from side to side, back and forth, as if she's surveying the motionless pirates lying slain about the deck, as if she's shaking her head "no."

Seeing Matthew again I realized I can't be the Wendy anymore. I don't want to be the woman-part in a hetero pair. I can no longer be the one who waits behind in her bedroom, who has to grow old, into a woman— who has to learn to speak the way Alex did over the internet to those strangers / who has to move her hips when she walks like I used to / who has to wear her hair long / who has to figure out how to use the right bathroom / who has to be scared of her own voice because she's scared of what people will see when they look at her, when they see the art she creates—while Peter gets to remain a boy.

*

My friend's mom sees my shaved head for the first time. She's known me for some time with my long hair and dresses and makeup. She tells me I still look like a beautiful girl. She really says this: *a beautiful girl*. I want to tell her about how, recently, every person I see looks like they're wearing a costume of gender. I have never seen it so clearly, how each cosmetic decision is meant to convey something—even if the individual has never thought of themself as anything but whatever they were told they were when they were born—I see their choices, which they make consciously or unconsciously every day as they move through the world. These choices are as definite as Betty Bronson's short hair under her pointed cap or the way, in the silent film, she moves so confidently, joyfully, like a little boy, around Wendy's room, eventually striding into the frame of the open window, stretching out her arms, and flying up and away to Neverland. There, she can be a boy forever.

steamboat

Buses of tourists unload in parking lots to swarm boardwalks over hot, bubbling earth. P and I circle the wooden walkways with the masses. We're on a road trip from New Orleans through the West to California. Yellowstone is the only national park I've been to that feels more like a theme park than nature. Early in the morning, it's cold and clouds of sulfur envelop us—small children make a show of holding their noses. Couples ask strangers to take pictures of them in front of an impossibly blue steaming lake rimmed with rust. P and I trade off my Nikon; we take photos of the landscape, which won't be as impressive as reality, in black and white. One of the pools sits in the ground like a dark wound. The water is clear, and I need to know so badly how deep the darkness goes. When I stare into the deadly gurgling mud pits and pools of scalding water, I feel an urge to submerge myself Jacuzzi-style. It reminds me of how, when I stand atop a very tall building and look down, I'm scared of the space between my body and the ground, not because of the height but because my body aches to experience it—drawn to the edge, part of me wants to know what it's like to fall. Now, I consciously pull myself back onto the boardwalk, away from my confusing desires.

*

In her essay "My Dangerous Desires," political organizer and lesbian sex radical Amber L. Hollibaugh writes, "No gender system is natural, no system of desire organic or removed from the way culture creates human experience. We are raised to become 'masculine' or 'feminine,' and any rebellion against that still takes place within a constructed system of gender and erotic binaries—at least in white America."

*

Around the time my parents met, my dad passed through Yellowstone several times on his road trips between college in Connecticut and his home in San Francisco. I only recently found out my dad once shared my love of long-distance drives and roadside adventures. He too hiked and camped and met strange people along the way. He was even a park ranger at Sunset Crater in Arizona for a summer. We never went camping when I was growing up—my siblings and I were city kids through and through—because my mom was never really into the outdoors. The narrative, as I understood it, was that my dad was the adventurous one, the wild one.

This idea of him, at least, is why my mom had initially been drawn to him. My dad grew up in San Francisco during the '60s and, despite having been too young to really participate, he had certainly been molded by the counterculture. He started smoking weed when he was eleven, even once smoking with his teachers in middle school, and his parents let him roam free with no nightly curfews. One of his sisters was a Deadhead—though admittedly late to the trend, in the '70s—while the other moved to New York City and became entrenched in the Lower East Side scene, her friends artists and heroin addicts.

In comparison my mom's childhood in Burbank had been suffocating—when I picture it, the images are always shrouded in a dark cigarette haze, the blinds drawn all day. Both of her parents were uptight and fervent alcoholics. My mom was not permitted to leave the house unless she had a boyfriend, which she didn't, so she spent most of her evenings as a teenager stuck at home. The wholesomeness the Disney company is known for is wedded with conservativeness, with a *waiting for your prince to come* kind of mentality, and—with her dad continuing to work at the company his father, Roy, and Uncle Walt founded—this was the environment my mom was raised in. She desperately needed to break away from this existence. She fell in love with a boy she met in college, a guy with a mop of wild brown curls, the drummer in a sloppy punk band, someone unpredictable, to make a new kind of life.

*

At one of the wooden platforms in Yellowstone, P and I come across a few people sitting on foldout camping chairs, reading books in the hot midday sun. We discover they are waiting for the Steamboat Geyser to explode. Steamboat is a larger geyser than Old Faithful, its powerful stream reaching around 300 feet into the air, compared to Old Faithful's average 130–140 feet. While Old Faithful was named for the fact that it reliably blows every hour or so—now for crowds of hundreds seated on bleachers like an hourly stage show at Disney World—Steamboat's eruptions are highly unpredictable. Sometimes, days will pass between explosions, and at other times, years. A group of only ten or so wait around for it. P and I sit on a bench and watch Steamboat shoot small streams of boiling water sideways from its depths. We ponder aloud if these smaller eruptions mean it might blow soon.

Next to us is a pale-faced teenage boy in a camping chair, sitting alone. He wears a large-brimmed fishing hat and reads a Kindle. *How long have you been here?* P asks him. P is often the more outgoing of the two of us, having grown up in the South, where it's normal for people to strike up conversations with random strangers. (Maybe this is normal most places—I just grew up in Manhattan, where it's definitely not). *Since Sunday*, the boy replies. *But I have been here a total of twenty-eight days in my lifetime*, he continues, and his tone has a mathematic precision. When he speaks he holds his hands out with his fingers extended and palms flattened, moving them back and forth as if weighing something invisible between them. *I have been here a total of twenty-eight days but I've never seen it,* and with these words my heart aches for this boy. I admire him, how he keeps coming back. We are greedy, P and I, to think we deserve this show.

*

I fear my abbreviated version of my mom's upbringing undercuts the reality. In her childhood home, there was a great deal of male rage, along with an understanding that women were not permitted to dream. Instead, women were to be devoted advocates of their husbands' dreams. My mom recently told me about how her grandpa, Roy, filed a suit against the United States government arguing he should be able to write off his wife as a business expense on his taxes—he won. I'm not always sure, though, that these are my stories to tell.

*

New Orleans, this small city, feels so big right now. I round each corner, enter each coffee shop, each bar, wondering if they will be there. I stay out later at parties, hoping to see them. When I drive down Esplanade, I search the bike lane for their forms balancing on metal frames, as I estimate this would be their route home from work. I've never been to their homes though. I'm not even sure where, exactly, they live. For months we didn't have each other's numbers and we could rely on our common worlds to run into each other. Now I want to see them, hope to see them, and I don't; my religion, coincidence, is failing me.

*

When I was growing up, my mom spoke often to me and my siblings of her feminist ideals. When I was ten, for example, she took me and my sister out of school for a day to go to Washington DC to walk in a pro-choice march. My sister and I were encouraged to see the world through a lens that emphasized our ability to choose and live our lives for ourselves. (Ironically, this is also why my mom kept the complicated last name as her own.) Still, we had all the Disney classics on VHS—they came to us, in the mail, from the company without our asking, new films and reeditions—and over and over again I watched *Snow White, Cinderella, Sleeping Beauty, Aladdin, Beauty and the Beast, The Little Mermaid,* and so on. The carefully crafted fairy-tale narratives pulled me in each time, and the songs filled me with hope and excitement. (They still do.) I especially loved Ariel and how she longs for a different reality than the one she's living. She wants a life above water, a new perspective. For Ariel, even though she's a princess, feet are what really represent freedom—without them, how could she jump, dance, stand on her own? Yet, like those other classics, Ariel's pursuit of a different life gets tangled up with her pursuit of love. Ultimately, the women in these films, who all seek freedom in their own ways, realize they can only find that freedom in the arms of a prince. And no matter how much my mom professed to me that these were antiquated ideas, no matter how much I believed her, how could a part of me not be infected by the concept of a spell broken only by true love's kiss?

*

I'm scared I might be always seen in relation to the *famous* artists in my family who have come before me. The truth is the artists I've always looked up to are on my dad's side, the Hauser side. My Nonna, his mother, is a painter and my aunt, his sister, is a visual artist and used to be a dancer. My dad is a writer and photographer. Nonna gave me my first drawing books and charcoal pencils; my aunt always gave me her old clothes, so I could pretend to be a punk in middle school in her worn Psychotic Pineapple shirt with the sleeves cut off; my dad gave me books to escape into. These are the artists I come from, whose art I deeply admire, even though few know our names. Instead, people might point to my mom's side for my inspiration, saying I aspire to have an imagination like Walt's, mistakenly thinking this lineage is the one that speaks to me—because he's the one who *really did it*, who got so famous for his art. And I guess, in a way, they're right. After all here I am, still writing about a man I didn't even know, who died twenty-five years before I was born.

*

When P and I started hooking up, I didn't want to date him. I made this clear. I didn't want to date anybody. I was enjoying my messy life in New Orleans—bartending, drinking all the time, living in a shotgun house with four roommates, talking about making films but never really following through with anything—and I wanted to continue throwing myself at other people. But P and I kept seeing each other for months and months and then, one day, I realized I didn't want to be anywhere else but with him. He made me laugh with his dry humor, the way he saw the world, how he wanted to crack open his understanding of life, like I did. We became best friends, who moved across the country together three times. We stumbled through our twenties, trying to figure out what we were going to do with our lives, finally settling back in New Orleans to both work in film. Our somewhat unromantic beginnings perhaps made the idea of an open relationship seem more possible even if most of the time we were happy to just be, together.

*

P and I leave Yellowstone, continuing toward San Francisco, where we plan to visit Nonna. I keep thinking about the boy waiting for Steamboat—his unwavering patience, his faith in unpredictability. *If he sees it erupt this time,* I ask P in the car as we drive through the dry flatness of Northern Nevada, *will he keep coming back? Will he want to see it again, even if it means waiting, again?* I look up the Steamboat Geyser on my phone and find out it erupted the day before, during the hour we packed our campsite and left Yellowstone—we must've been too close to the border of the park, at that point, to hear the loud churning of water into sky. The boy must've finally seen it, P and I agree, as he told us he planned to be at Yellowstone, posted up at Steamboat, for the rest of the week. But—what if he'd taken a break, I suggest, walking the forty or so feet down the boardwalk, away from the geyser, into the small cabin containing the bathrooms? What if he missed the moment of its actual eruption? I feel certain, whether he saw it erupt or not, that the boy would go back to wait again.

*

Let's keep things confused for a while, my dad supposedly said to my mom the morning after they made out the first time during their sophomore year of college. The other day on the phone, my mom told me they were coming up on the fortieth anniversary of that night; though, for the past eight months, they've been living in separate apartments. My mom said she'd joked to my dad that, forty years later, they were continuing to keep things confusing.

*

I have been taught, as a filmmaker, to show you, instead of telling you, why I feel the way I do. Why the thought runs loops in my mind: *I could never be a legitimate artist*—why this makes me so anxious. In America fame is a difficult substance to scrub off, especially when a name comes to have a life of its own, after the person who made the name known is dead. But fame cannot be worn again by descendants like a hand-me-down, passed down through the generations; the wearer will always change its meaning. My mom will never be Walt, never Roy, but in the articles written about her, her name is always followed by theirs. (After that, sometimes, she's described as a filmmaker.) No matter what, her identity will always have to do with them. Some refuse to believe Walt is actually gone, insisting he's cryogenically frozen and will come back someday—it's a joke, an urban legend, but I am shocked by how many people still believe this. How bizarre it is to carry this man with me, everywhere I go, a man who would see me as a stranger. I can feel him there every time Disney comes up in conversation, which happens laughably often. I'm either with people who know my middle name, and we can joke about it, or I'm with people who don't, and I pretend to be someone else, who hears *Disney* as a brand and not a weird extension of family. I pretend the word doesn't make my stomach turn a little each time I hear it. In these situations I question whether I should admit more readily that, like my mom, my identity will always have something to do with these dead men. If not admitting this is a form of dishonesty.

And now I carry my mom too—her name appearing more and more in the credits of the films I watch, the magazines I read, the websites I visit daily—and somehow this is heavier because, having experienced this all her life, she must know it's happening. But how could she stop it? How could I possibly ask her to stop wanting to be seen when that's a piece of what I want for myself? To be seen, at least, as separate from those in my family I carry.

*

The truth is, I don't know what I am. I don't want to have to pick, one or the other—I want to float, to exist in the in-between, inside the world of unpredictability. I don't want to be placed into a category of gender. I want my relationship to live here too, in this space between borders, between the boundaries of flesh that supposedly separate our bodies. I don't know what I want, or who I want, and this not-knowing is my only stability.

*

"Although do I write as a form of disappearance, or as a reaction against disappearance?" Kate Zambreno muses in a short piece about Elena Ferrante and notoriety as a writer in her collection *Screen Tests*. Zambreno's question springs from her discussion of the fact that her in-laws will never think of her as a writer and, in a sense, this is a form of comfort—she never has to worry about them reading what she's written. Does my mom make films to be forgotten? Do we write, my dad and I, to be forgotten? My dad also has to carry this man, a man he isn't even related to by blood, a madness he married into. To be in a relationship with someone with a famous last name, before you are old enough to establish yourself as a writer or whatever you wanted to be, is probably not unlike having the name yourself. The name plays tricks on all of us, letting us glimpse what it would be like to have the fame ourselves, so close we can almost feel its inexplicable significance within our bodies, without ever really touching it. It feels odd to really acknowledge it, to put it into words, but to be so close to what others deem important—for this to be an unalterable aspect of your identity—is to be reminded every day of your unimportance. Perhaps, then, in my family we write, we make films, to remind ourselves this proximity is not the only thing that defines us.

*

I want to create art that's unpredictable. I want to create art that imagines a new way of being instead of upholding the one that exists, that's accepted. Art that deviates from the way culture, the way Disney, creates human experience. I want to create myself, a person who recognizes their lineage but is not defined by it. I say this but I don't know how; I don't know if it's possible. So I will write.

*

My mom used to tell us all the time that she didn't believe in fairy tales, but she kind of did. Or, at least, she believed in the kind of love that lasts forever, even though such an ideal had not been modeled by her own parents—even though it's modeled by so few, perhaps only in the movies. I will admit, though, it is strange to continue on in a relationship if you always hold with you the awareness that it will end. But at the same time this unpredictability is what makes the state of my relationship with P so unbelievable. Each day we are still together, each day we are together at all, is a strange miracle. Especially when it feels like, sometimes, we are trying to explode it.

*

When I'm writing, I feel like that teenage boy at Yellowstone. I'm waiting for the inspiration to burst forth, not knowing if it will be days or months or years. This is what's so painful about making art, about relationships, about living—waiting, wanting, not knowing what will happen, but continuing to sit each day in your camping chair to patiently watch. Some days, the blankness of the page in front of me is unbearable. Some days, I wonder if P keeps texting that girl he slept with, keeps seeing her and flirting with her, if he will fall in love with her. If we continue this open relationship, could I fall in love with someone else? I don't know if there's anything I can do but wait.

*

When P and I were in Yellowstone and I found out about the Steamboat Geyser, I first thought of New Orleans. The city held by the brown curve of the Mississippi River and, atop it, the Steamboat Natchez, a floating tourist attraction where several of my friends work. The twinkling of the calliope carried on the wind to far reaches of the city. I thought of the steamboat itself, an invention that allowed for mass industrialization, the primary reason for levees—the infrastructure that locked the Mississippi River in place and made it into the nation's central vein of commerce and capitalism.

Then I thought of Steamboat Willie. Hand-drawn Mickey in black and white, tapping his foot and whistling as he steers the boat rapidly down the River. The small vessel's smokestacks rhythmically coughing black clouds into the sky. These are the images that made my life into this dream I will keep trying to make sense of.

ashes

Slowly we crept, the line winding around itself, toward the Haunted Mansion with its Gothic-revival exterior, fake tombstones set in grass surrounding the abandoned estate. After we waited in line for some time, a big group of us was ushered into the candlelit entryway. On the striped walls of the octagonal room were large painted portraits. When the whole room began to move—since it's actually a functional elevator—the portraits stretched to unveil disturbing continuations of their original images. A painting of a woman with a parasol stretched to reveal she's actually standing on a tightrope above the wide-open jaws of a hungry-eyed alligator (a fright that now seems a little close to home at Disney World). Then the room went completely dark, and lightning flashed, briefly exposing a body hanging from the rafters above. I was twenty-seven, but that hanging body still gave me the creeps. The doors opened on the other end of the room, and we walked in a line, through a large hallway, onto a moving walkway. From there we boarded plastic armchairs, "Doombuggies" the recorded narrator called them, which would transport us through the ride.

At the time I had a vague memory of a guide at Disney World telling me and my siblings that one of the characters on the Haunted House ride was modeled in the likeness of our great-grandfather, Roy. Or after our grandfather, also named Roy—I couldn't remember which. Because of this, I'd always regarded a particular singing hologram statue in the graveyard portion of the ride with a level of reverence incongruous with the setting.

That night on the ride, my plastic chair swiveled backward to signal we were moving into the graveyard, where everything glows in black light. Projections of ghostly figures flew across the fake night sky. Animatronic skeletons attempted to burst from their graves. Then, once again, I saw the hologram of my deceased family member. The statue bust that most resembles my dead grandpa sings gleefully along to the spooky music with a group of other statue busts, smiling in a manner I never saw my grandpa smile. The image has always been scarier to me than anything else on the Haunted House ride.

*

My grandparents, Roy and Patty Disney, announced their engagement at the opening party for Disneyland in 1955. They had four kids in the four following years, my mom the third. They raised them in a wealthy suburban area of Burbank called Toluca Lake, a location favored by my family because of its proximity to the Disney studios. Each day my grandfather would drive approximately eight minutes to his office at the animation department, which he was the head of for many years. For some time, his office was located in the huge blue *Fantasia*-style sorcerer's hat adorning the top of the animation building (a building that, after his death, is now emblazoned with his own name). When I was a child, we went to visit my grandfather at his office a few times. I remember so well that conical room, a huge desk at the center. He ultimately had to move out of the hat to a different office because the slanted walls were giving him vertigo.

*

I exited the Haunted House ride, regaining my balance after stepping off the moving walkway, striding back out into the night air, fireworks popping loudly overhead. Again, I thought of my inability to place the strange memory about the bust.

I found a place to sit on the ground. Cross-legged on cement, I pulled out my phone so I could scour the Disney-obsessed websites and blogs for information to confirm this family legend. Ultimately, though, I found nothing. Our guide would not have been misinformed, as guides take their knowledge of the park very seriously, so perhaps my mom told me this weird fact about her father. She's a very intelligent woman who's still been known to get things wrong, stating with authority all kinds of information I've repeated to others only to find myself corrected and embarrassed. She even admits this about herself: she's a *don't let facts get in the way of a good story* kind of woman, who also gets a particular kick out of shocking her listener.

A more probable explanation, however, is that *I* dreamt the fact—I dreamt the whole situation of a guide telling us about our grandfather on the Haunted House ride—and remembered it as reality. I'm realizing, reluctantly, I've inherited this trait from my mom (and maybe, in part, this is where my inclination toward storytelling comes from).

Through my internet searching, though, I soon discovered the bust I believed to be my grandpa was actually modeled after Thurl Ravenscroft, famous for singing the Mr. Grinch theme song and for voicing Tony the Tiger; however, the bust had long been incorrectly identified by park-goers as Walt Disney. Around me crowds rushed to get a better view of the fireworks. I sat on warm ground and felt slightly affirmed by the many others who thought the bust was Walt—since my grandpa looked like his uncle, it seemed appropriate for me to consider that singing hologram statue as if it were an actual ghost. Perhaps we can conjure reality by simply believing.

*

"Current and former custodians at Disney parks say identifying and vacuuming up human ashes is a signature and secret part of working at the
Happiest Place on Earth," wrote Erich Schwartzel in a 2018 article for the
Wall Street Journal.[1] Recently, through this news item, I discovered I was
not the only one to feel the presence of familial spirits on the Haunted
House ride. According to park workers, the Haunted House is the most
popular site for this ritual, which Schwartzel's interviewees claim is the
ultimate way to honor deceased family members who were big fans of the
park. Apparently, "HEPA cleanups," Disney's code word for vacuuming
human remains, are required about once a month. Schwartzel posits
that since Disney World is considered by some a place of many rites—
proposals, birthdays, and marriages—it's not entirely surprising "some
want to spend eternity there." One woman, who sprinkled her mother's
ashes into the water on the "It's a Small World" ride, told Schwartzel she
commemorates the anniversary of her mother's passing not by going to
a cemetery, but by going to Disney World.

*

When my grandfather Roy died of stomach cancer, five separate memorial services were held for him. I flew with my parents and siblings to
Los Angeles to attend the three memorials there. I was eighteen.

1.   The wake—as I think it was called, though my grandfa-
      ther's body was not present—was at the residence of one
      of my uncles in Toluca Lake, houses away from where my
      grandparents had lived almost all their lives and where my
      grandmother still lived. I remember my uncle, also named
      Roy, warning his youngest son not to bring up our grand-
      father's death to our grandmother. Her Alzheimer's was
      worsening, and no one knew how to explain the situation to
      her yet. Soon before his death, my grandfather had left my
      grandmother and their fifty-two-year marriage for a younger
      woman, a woman who'd also dated my uncle many years
      before. In her state my grandma was basically unable to

process this monumental shift in her life. She still referred to my grandpa as her husband and often wondered aloud where he was. That night at the wake, my grandma entered the room, and immediately my small cousin, Roy's son, ran to her, exclaiming, "Grandpa died!" My grandma paused and we all sucked in our breaths. Then she calmly intoned, "Yes—he did it well, didn't he?" and continued to the appetizers.

2. My grandpa's ashes were first spread during a memorial on the water in Newport Beach. That day the "Pyewacket," a sailboat he'd raced for many years, to Hawaii and elsewhere, contained close friends and family members (including the *new wife*, Irene, to my mom's and her siblings' dismay). Several sailboats with other mourners cruised alongside us. I remember one of my aunts, only recently married to my uncle, wearing an incredibly short skirt, a tight shirt showcasing her perfect, possibly fake breasts, and flip-flop heels—an outfit I knew some of my family members were sure to be scandalized by, which I found somewhat hilarious. I remember throwing flower leis into the Pacific Ocean and the sandy feeling of ashes, carried on the wind, somehow, into my slightly ajar mouth, the sickening grit of my grandfather on my teeth.

3. The company memorial for my grandfather was at a theater on the Hollywood strip across from the famous Chinese Theatre. A large crowd, wearing Hawaiian shirts in honor of him—as, I guess, he was known to wear Hawaiian shirts—filtered into the huge theater and took their seats. Then ensued a variety-show-style tribute to my grandfather, a man I quickly realized I knew even less about than I originally thought. An Irish step-dance team performed, and Dick Van Dyke said a few words. Jodi Benson, the woman who voiced the original Little Mermaid, sang "Part of Your World." A man who played Mufasa on Broadway sang "He Lives in You," a song from *The Lion King* musical about the great kings of the past continuing to live on through Simba, watching over everything he does. Some

preppy-looking people around my age, former crewmembers on my grandpa's sailboat, took the stage and talked about how Roy was "like a grandfather to them." I remember leaving the darkness of the theater that sunny afternoon with a headache, wanting to burst out laughing at the absurdity of the cheesy songs and the gaudy, high-production-value performances but knowing this wouldn't be the appropriate behavior of a grand-kid. How was this the same man who'd left my grandmother as soon as she started showing signs her memory was slipping? For the first time, I realized what could happen when fam-ily mythology and national mythology bleed into each other, rendering one incapable of knowing who their ancestors really were—their flaws censored for the sake of a brand image.

*

On Mardi Gras day, I usually spend the morning costumed and slowly following the clumsy movements of the St. Anne's parade. The parade begins in the Bywater and moves through the Marigny, all the way across the French Quarter, then loops around and ends near Jackson Square at the River's edge. There, as the brass band plays "Down by the River-side," folks in wild costumes toss the ashes of their recently deceased loved ones into the Mississippi River. Formed in the '60s, many of the original members of the Secret Society of Saint Anne were gay bohemi-ans and, when their friend group was devastated by the AIDS epidemic, their Mardi Gras parade became an annual funeral for those they'd lost that year.[2] Now, you don't have to be a part of the society to participate; hundreds trail along with the parade, some just to dance along with the band, and others to participate in its final ritual. Since my first St. Anne's parade, I've always loved the idea of my friends or family members or whomever, faces painted, covered in glitter, drunkenly stumbling with the brass band's music to the River, throwing my ashes, however unceremoniously, into the brown water. I can completely understand, therefore, the desire of some to be scattered at Disney World. There is something joyful about the idea—a sense of humor, an eagerness to challenge how we mourn. Perhaps most of all, I appreciate those who spread their family members' ashes on the Haunted House ride, a goofy place that parodies death and our fears of it. I love these people, sprinkling their mom, their grandfather, under the black light, amidst the animatronic ghosts and other theatrics of the Haunted House ride, encouraging the dead to remain there forever, laughing at the living.

Both the St. Anne's parade and the custom of scattering ashes at Disney World honor the specificity of the deceased as they were in life. Funerals, much like weddings, often adhere to expectations of tradition, sometimes to an extent that the ceremony can feel more like watching a film than an actual event you're experiencing. When everything is following the same script as always, you start to wonder if you really knew the person being eulogized—or married—or if perhaps you fabricated the relationship you'd had with them, completely misinterpreting the facts of their personality.

The most recent funeral I attended was at a Catholic church in Northern Ireland, and the sermon was given by a priest who had not actually known my family friend, Molly, in life. He gave a sweet sermon, reciting details about her sense of humor and her idiosyncratic turns of phrase, which someone close to Molly must have told him, but it still seemed strange to me that he had never met her. Molly's husband, Tom, gave a brief speech then played on a stereo a piece of classical music they used to listen to together, sitting in their living room in rural County Cork. Molly and Tom were in their late fifties and didn't have any children. I'd never seen two people who loved to be in each other's company more, and her untimely death broke my heart. After the ceremony Molly's male relatives carried the casket out of the church, through cold rain, into the small, adjacent graveyard, and her large family gathered around as they put her into the ground. The ceremony was moving and probably quite representative of the culture Molly had grown up in. It was also, in some ways, very stiff and sad in a manner so wholly unrelated to the perpetually ecstatic and hilarious Molly.

After the funeral there was a reception at the local sports pavilion, and I ate soup with my three siblings and cried quietly. As my dad, siblings, and I were leaving the reception, we ran into Tom, who invited us to come to a pub for a pint with him and some of Molly's family members. At first my dad refused, not wanting to intrude on their family mourning, but Tom insisted. At the pub we got beers with Tom, his siblings, and a few of Molly's nieces and nephews. Two of her nephews, in their late twenties, made sure my underage brother got a beer—*yeah right, it's your first drink*. They laughed and teased him in their charming Irish accents. Tom pointed out a small photo, pinned up above the bar, of an old lady with white hair. *Molly's mum*, he explained. He found it a very comical location for her commemorative portrait to hang, as Molly's mom had been sober her whole life.

We told stories about Molly and laughed, and I was sorry I was just getting to know her family in this way—I wished so badly I could tell her how much I liked them. A little tipsy, we walked out of the warm bar back into the cold, gray day, the smell of manure hanging in the air, and hugged Tom goodbye on the sidewalk. *I feel like I'm on acid*, I said to Tom. *I know what you mean*, Tom agreed and then, laughing, immediately corrected himself, *I mean, what is that like?* Tom is American, but his voice has picked up a distinctly Irish musicality from spending so many years in the country and living with Molly for so long. Walking back to the car, I was glad we'd gone to the bar with him. The convening felt like another memorial.

*

A year ago Jon drove me and Lara around Pointe-aux-Chenes and the surrounding bayou towns in his massive lifted pickup truck with 37-inch tires. As we moved I felt like we were drifting, unmoored, above the winding roads. We were doing research for a documentary Lara was directing and had driven over an hour from New Orleans to the frayed tip of Louisiana to meet Jon, a friend of a friend and a Cajun local. Being a fixer for films was one of Jon's many hustles, along with alligator hunting,

DJ-ing, and renting airboats, so he'd volunteered to be our tour guide for the day. We drove past stilted houses and stretches of water Jon told us had been grassy cow pastures when he was a kid. He recounted what growing up here, in a sinking landscape, was like. He talked about his family, pointing out relatives' houses as we passed them.

As we got closer to Jon's house, the road began to snake parallel to a thin green bayou. Live oaks melted with Spanish moss over the still water. He was telling us his sister refused to eat the deer he hunted. *Don't kill Bambi!* Jon imitated his sister and laughed. Just then his phone rang, a jarring cackle erupting loudly from his Android—a familiar sound to me since Jon's phone had been ringing all day, but only in that moment did I recognize the ringtone's origins. My grandfather could do the sound impeccably; it came from his lips and made me smile: Donald Duck's laugh. My grandpa not only looked a little like his Uncle Walt, he also had a similar voice, so he could do those impressions well—it's one of the few things I remember about him.

I was a very anxious child, my shyness almost debilitating, so my grandfather was largely a stranger to me. He was intimidating, patriarchal in a way my father wasn't, and our being related didn't make a difference to me—it didn't make it easier for me to talk to him. I don't remember ever interacting with him one-on-one. I saw my grandparents rarely, when we went to LA for a big family event or when they came to New York every other year for a Disney film premiere.

What I know about my grandfather is a hazy mixture of my mom's stories, information from the internet, and my imagination:

1. My grandfather was the head of the Disney animation department for many years, overseeing the studio during the "renaissance" period, when they produced hits such as *The Little Mermaid, Beauty and the Beast,* and *The Lion King.* He was known for questioning the company's top managers when

he felt they were leading the company astray from the vision of his forebears. Over the years he led several campaigns to oust executives of the company, including forcing the 1984 resignation of Ron Miller, the husband of Walt's daughter Diane.[3]

2. My grandfather was the last member of the Disney family to work at the company.

3. When my mom and her siblings were growing up, my grandpa would come home from work each day, settle into his armchair, and chain smoke, often drinking himself into a rage-fueled stupor. Once, when my mother was twelve and had a friend over, she disobeyed her father in some way, disrupting his cocktail hour with their young laughter. He pulled her pants down and spanked her in front of her friend, shame stinging red on her bare ass.

4. According to his obituary in the *New York Times*, when he was a boy, my grandfather would play in the halls of the animation department, and the animators often asked him to be a test audience for films they were working on, like *Pinocchio*. The obituary ends: *Mr. Disney was a big fan of referring to the past to define the future. He told a biographer: "The goal is to look over our shoulder and see Snow White and Pinocchio and Dumbo standing there saying, 'Be this good.' We shouldn't be intimidated by them; they're an arrow pointing someplace."*

5. Recently, my mom told me that when she was in her twenties, after graduating from college, she went back to LA to help her dad at the company. She'd always been ambitious and very smart, an "overachiever" to her family. Her father told her he didn't want her help. He didn't say so directly but it was clear—she was a woman, unqualified to uphold the family name. Instead, he gave both of her brothers jobs, which neither of them ended up keeping very long.

Attending my grandfather's memorials was very different from my experience of Molly's funeral. I was close to Molly. I knew who we were mourning—I knew how the methods of mourning reflected or didn't reflect Molly. In the case of my grandfather, I felt I was learning about the man through his death, while also remaining skeptical of this portrayal.

Molly had become like an aunt to me because I'd seen her every year since I was a baby, when my extended family would go to Ireland for several weeks each summer. Molly and her husband, Tom, were the caretakers of my grandparents' castle in County Cork—how long I've told friends I was going to my grandparents' "house" in Ireland (though my grandparents were never there when we went), hoping to invoke in the listener's mind the image of a quaint thatch-roofed cabin, sitting unassumingly in a green field dotted with dirty sheep. Molly and Tom lived year-round in a house beside the castle, attached to the main house by the large stone wall that surrounds the back gardens. When I was young, they babysat for my siblings, my cousins, and me. They sat us on their laps and played games with us, watched movies with us in their living room, helped us make animals out of poster board to place in the forest surrounding the property so we could pretend it was a jungle. They marked their kitchen door with notches, names, and ages, to document how much we'd grown over the years. As I got older, Molly and Tom's became a place to escape my cousins when they were teasing me, or my mom when she was not understanding me. I would go to their warm kitchen, and they'd give me a cup of Barry's tea and make jokes that made me laugh so hard, reminding me to take myself less seriously.

*

Recently, I was in Los Angeles for a three-day lab for independent film producers based in the South. During the short trip, we had endless networking meetings with industry professionals to pitch our projects. The lab had been funded by 20th Century Fox and, since the company had recently been acquired by Disney, we unexpectedly had to attend a group meeting with executives at Disney Studios. No one in the program knew my relation, so I went to the meeting inadvertently undercover. I was surprised by how familiar the place was, even though I hadn't been in many years, since my grandfather's death. We drove past the big blue sorcerer's hat to the front entrance of the studios, which I recognized, remembering the huge beige building with sculptures of the seven dwarves holding up the roof like columns. We received our name tags, "Chachi Hauser" next to a cheerful Mickey and well-known script that read "The Walt Disney Company." I walked, silently, with the group of young producers through the hallways, past black-and-white pictures of my relatives.

In a large, plain-looking boardroom, we sat nervously around an oval table as the executives talked to us about their diversity initiatives, their search for "fresh blood" and "the next *Modern Family*." In describing Disney's new streaming service, they explained to us the difference between Disney brands, like FX and ESPN, and Disney-branded—calling to mind the origin of the term, it was hard for me not to think of my family name seared into flesh—meaning content with the name "Disney" attached to it, which is obligated to fulfill the "brand promise." One executive, who was originally an employee of 20th Century Fox and clearly not thrilled about her new position, told us with palpable bitterness that Disney was, as always, looking for uplifting narratives that satisfied the "four quadrants" (husband, wife, son, and daughter). Like robots, the other executives reiterated the most significant elements of the Disney brand promise: heroism, warmth, positivity, hopefulness, family.

*

The male name "Roy" is often defined as meaning "king." My great-grandfather, Walt's brother, passed this name down to his son who, in turn, did the same, this cycle repeating itself such that my eldest cousin is the fourth man in my family named Roy. If he has children, I'm sure my cousin will feel obligated to name his first male offspring the same.

When the larger storytelling consciousness intersects so distinctly with one's personal reality, this distorts your sense of self, and this identity alienates you. Perhaps this had made my grandfather feel both overly important and deeply insignificant all at once.

Walt had two daughters, no sons. I've never known how much of a choice Walt's nephew, my grandfather, had to live another life.

It's so fucking corny, but the song "He Lives in You" still finds its way into my skull sometimes and won't leave. I think about him watching over everything I see, the water as the truth—how he supposedly lives in my reflection.

*

When I first moved to New Orleans, I worked for a year as a bartender at a hotdog joint on Frenchmen Street. There, I fell briefly and madly in love with one of the cooks. Grant had a nose ring and black, mullet-like hair and a tattoo of a pentagram on his inner wrist. He was from Monroe, Louisiana. He was perpetually frowning as he sweated over the grill, but he had these big, sexy eyes with long black lashes. The sound of him angrily snapping his tongs from across the restaurant never failed to make me swoon. For the hottest months of summer, Grant and I made out in the supply closet at work and had clumsy drunk sex, always at my house because he still lived in a cramped studio apartment with his ex-girlfriend. We worked until 5:00 a.m. and smoked cigarettes on my rusty balcony until the sun came up, and told each other we loved each other even though we knew it was dumb.

Grant told me about his mother, who was in and out of rehab with a drug addiction, and about his experiences traveling the country, panhandling, and about all the other lives he had lived. He told me about his heroin problem. I didn't tell him much about my parents or my upbringing. My mom retained her last name when she married my dad but allowed her children the option of hiding, making her last name our middle name and purposefully deciding against hyphenation. When I went to Ireland for a week that summer, I didn't explain to Grant I'd been many times before or where in Ireland, exactly, I was going. I saw him being vulnerable, raw, but I didn't allow him to see me this way. Soon, we fell apart, messily: as it turned out, we were both sleeping with other people. I wrote in my journal: *It is terrifying to realize how much of a disappointment you can be, to understand how much contradiction you're capable of.* In my relationships, I can create a dynamic of dishonesty, allowing others to expose themselves to me while never giving them the same nakedness in return.

*

In my grandparents' castle, I find a binder full of copies of old deeds and newspaper articles about the property. A clipping from the October 15th, 1989, issue of an Irish paper called *The Sunday Press* contains the headline "The Disney Empire's Foot-hold in Ireland" beneath a big photo of my grandpa in front of the castle. Overlaid on the larger photo is a picture of Walt and Mickey Mouse. The article begins, "When Roy Disney was a child, his classmates would ask if Goofy was modeled on him. Nephew of Walt, Roy may have obvious ears—but he's no Goofy." The clipping is cut off there, so I can't see what follows that short first paragraph. In reading this, I feel a closeness to my grandpa I've never experienced before. I know this form of teasing well, about being called, unimaginatively, "Walt" by loudmouthed guys in high school corridors. I know about rolling your eyes or laughing along. I know about learning to make the joke before someone else can; learning to tell them about how, for example, on my dad's first trip to my mom's family home, when they were in college, he checked their freezer for Walt, cheekily referencing the myth that he was cryogenically frozen.

I also know how, even when the teasing stops, friends and acquaintances will mention to you anything Disney they come across—how a friend you've lost touch with suddenly reaches out, sending pictures from his trip to Disney World, or how a news article about the latest Disney acquisition finds its way into your inbox from an ex-lover. I'm familiar with the fact that, to some—certainly to those I haven't seen in years, who might've otherwise forgotten me—I will be only this association. I realize now my grandpa must've been followed by this all his life and he had no way of hiding. His name, his looks, and his continued involvement in the business had rendered him unable to ever escape the jokes, the comparisons. His life was an extension of his father's life, his uncle's life. Maybe buying a castle was my grandpa's very extravagant attempt to own the joke.

A page later in the binder there's another newspaper clipping, this one with the headline "Disney graves discovered in Clonmesh." Someone—it looks like Molly's handwriting—has scribbled in pen at the edge of the clipping: *Thought Mrs. Disney would enjoy this.* "It has been discovered that direct ancestors of Walt Disney, king of cartoon film-makers, lie buried in a derelict, overgrown graveyard some three miles from Carlow Town." The article traces the forward lineage of the three deceased with the now well-known name, a line that moves awkwardly but directly to the "king of cartoon film-makers." Unknown, their bodies now earth in an allegedly forsaken graveyard in Ireland. These people are as closely related to the famous stranger as I am—the roots instead of the branches in his family tree.

On the other side of the binder page are photos of the three discovered headstones, and one photo is very familiar. Seeing it, I laugh, finally understanding the context for an image I've known for many years. When my mom turned forty, my grandparents sent her the photograph, printed large and framed—a close up of a headstone. My grandma's sense of humor did not land well that day as my mom, usually one for dark humor herself, was noticeably disturbed by the sight of her full name on a gravestone.

*

The December afternoon of my grandfather's third memorial, I sat in that dark theater on the Hollywood strip beside my siblings and cousins. A man from the company, maybe an animator, stood on stage with a mic and told a story about my grandfather that elicited laughter from the audience. The story involved my grandfather's refusal to put out a cigarette on a plane, despite the flight attendant's pleas for him to do so. The man who told the story found humor in my grandfather's stubbornness, a quality he seemed to admire. I grew more and more unnerved by the story, which seemed to be a model of my grandfather's entitlement, the more perverse aspects of which I'd heard about, throughout my life, from my mom. I'm sure he was drunk, belligerent, when this happened.

In a sense the story also made me feel sorry for him. A man who could not unearth himself from the legacy of his father and uncle, who was haunted by these men and how their lives would always overshadow his—I knew his entitlement had a lot to do with these feelings of inadequacy. But, at the same time, I sat there in the theater, imagining my grandfather in a cloud of smoke, the desperate, tired eyes of the flight attendant begging him to put the cigarette out, and all I could think was *what an asshole.*

*

After the memorials in Los Angeles, my mom flew with her three siblings and new stepmother, Irene, to Hawaii to spread the rest of her father's ashes. My dad, my siblings, and I went back to New York.

4. In Hawaii my mom, her siblings, and Irene spread some ashes while swimming together in the ocean. During this trip, relations were tense. My mom and her siblings were still adjusting to their mother's diagnosis, to their parents' separation, and to the concept of Irene as stepmother—now, she was in charge of the mourning process for their father. Still, they tried to be cool. They swam in the idyllic blue ocean, spreading ashes from their rationed Ziploc bags.

5. There was to be another formal ceremony—on sailboats in Hawaii—arranged by Irene and other folks, who my grandpa knew from the yacht club, that my mom had never met before. Staying in the same house together, everyone got dressed to

head to the final memorial. Just before leaving her room, my mom checked her email and read a message from the family lawyer. Before his death her father had rearranged his will, leaving everything to Irene, his wife of two years, and nothing to my grandmother. My mom came downstairs to find Irene in white, who explained she'd wear her wedding dress to the memorial—my mom laughs as she recounts this creepy detail. They all drove to the yacht club together and, when they arrived, my mom hid in the bathroom. She waited for the yacht club dining room to fall quiet, for all the sailboats to cast off, then she got a cab to the airport alone.

6. At the airport, realizing there was a small amount of ashes left in her Ziploc bag, my mom locked herself in a bathroom stall. She emptied the remnants of her father's ashes into the toilet, and flushed.

grand isle part I

When the Mississippi River was able to overflow and change course, it built up the land, depositing sediment, creating the ground we walk on, we build houses on, strip malls, highways. Now, my loneliness expands into the corners of our small apartment in New Orleans, settling into each room like layers of dust, flecks of skin. On Monday my mom called: she and my dad are separated again. Sunday morning I curl up in bed, phone to my face, scrolling through strangers on Tinder. P has been out of town for weeks, and I'm alone in the first apartment I've lived in without roommates. I don't message the internet possibilities—I don't know how I would tell them about P. I just flip through their pictures, faces receding before they can even make an impression, like glances from the windows of a passing subway train.

The River is restrained by levees, so we are sinking and each year the sea gets higher. I sink into the ugly brown couch in my living room and watch our three miniature shrimp on the coffee table, so tiny you can hardly see them. Their miniscule red forms swirl restlessly in the glass jar as if tossed by a fickle wind. They pick at something invisible with their legs along the distorted curvature. Too often I've had these kinds of pets, which can only be watched, never held or cuddled, like Maisy, the anxious, nocturnal hedgehog who lived beneath my bed in college.

I'd remove Maisy from her cage with a thick gardening glove, placing the spikey ball of her body on the carpet. I would wait as she slowly, cautiously, revealed herself.

No longer able to deposit it, the River spills its sediment out into the Gulf, and the U.S. Army Corps has to remove it, millions spent every year to dredge the mouth of the River—soft dirt prized in one area and worthless in another. They have to dredge so boats can enter and exit through the mouth, especially deep-sea vessels, which transport Louisiana's oil across the world. Barges with large tanks, viscous black liquid sloshing inside their metal bodies. Jess's big hands covered in bike grease, her British accent a surprising sound in Louisiana. The tattoo on her stomach I saw poking out from under her T-shirt a few weeks ago when we lay next to each other on the trampoline at our friends' house, a house I inhabited a few years ago, when I was younger and didn't live with P. I wrote a short film about that house, where I lived with four other dirty young people and two mangy cats. I used to be bursting with ideas for screenplays, every new person I met a character, every object a potential prop.

Humans turned the River into what they wanted it to be, deciding even a river has to have a function. Sunday morning turning into afternoon, I leave my creaky apartment, walk down the rusty metal stairs through the alleyway, into the French Quarter. Only a few blocks from my place, the narrow streets become dense with tourists. Their bodies move on sidewalks under the shade of wrought-iron balconies hanging with lush plants, recently watered and spilling onto the pavement below. These streets look nearly the same as when colonizers first decided to live with the River this way, when they decided to restrain it and forced enslaved people to build levees so they could find permanence on top of an alluvial plain. Monday, on the phone, my mom told me she left my dad in their 26th Street apartment and got a hotel room in Times Square for the week. She told me about her small, spare room, *almost monastic*, in a hotel where people from Jersey stay the night when they come to see

Kinky Boots. She wanted to feel as alone as possible, which is why she
came to 42nd, where you can feel like a ghost walking through all those
bodies, obliviously shuffling along and looking up, watching the bright
lights through their screens.

p loves me
i love him
over the four years we've been together i've felt something like love
for people who are not p
when p calls me from our home in new orleans to tell me he's slept
with someone else for the first time since we said   we loved each
other   i feel like i'm about to throw up   i also feel
strangely euphoric   my whole body turning inside out   i hang up on
him and blast robyn's "call your girlfriend" on my laptop and dance
around my hotel room and laugh because i'm the girlfriend who's
being called
i sent a text without thinking the day before   answering his question
yes   he could sleep with her   i didn't think he would really do it
the open relationship was my idea   i thought i wanted to have sex with
other people   but i was scared   if i did   i could fall in love with them

I wander down Royal Street. I buy a beer at a corner store and sip from
the can as I walk to the River. I sit on a bench at the Moon Walk and
watch massive barges slowly round the sharp corners of the brown river.
French tourists take photos in front of a plaque detailing the history of
the slave trade in New Orleans, and they're smiling too much in front
of these words to know what they mean. It's December but American
tourists are dressed like it's summer and carrying fishbowls containing vibrant cocktails, *hurricanes.* They document each other with their
phones as they suck pink liquid through ribbed straws.

If this were a movie, I would purposefully pop one of my bike tires just
so I could go see Jess at the bike shop where she works. I would keep
inventing bike problems just to go there, just to watch Jess's hands move

over my bike frame. If this were a movie, all my desires would have to be visualized that way, through action; my desires couldn't simply live in my head as they usually do. Maybe I should write a screenplay. Maybe I should try to form a story, an attempt to understand it: my renewed longing that for some reason I can't turn off but also can't act on. How, at the same time, my parents are breaking up again. But it takes so much time—to write a movie, to make it into something tangible—by the time it's watchable, I probably won't have the same feelings I wanted to make a movie about anymore.

P is working on my college friend James's feature film in Grand Isle, Louisiana's last inhabited barrier island, two hours away from New Orleans. Like the other barrier islands along Louisiana's coast, Grand Isle is a strip of land leftover, built up long ago when the River had a different path. There's no longer a River to maintain the land that once existed around Grand Isle, before it was an island, and now it's battered by storms, vulnerable and disappearing. From above you can see how Grand Isle and the other barrier islands form a border, like residual marks from a faded sketch of Louisiana's former shape. Having met him through me, James asked P to work on his film a few years ago. James had finally raised the money to turn the script into the regimented chaos that is a film set, and still I held onto an unspoken question: *why hadn't he asked me?* I knew I probably wasn't qualified—or perhaps I simply wasn't qualified because I didn't think I was—so P went down to Grand Isle without me.

In maps from the 1800s, the New Orleans area is referred to as an "isle" or an "island," surrounded by water on every side—the lakes, the gulf, the River, the wetlands. When I first moved to New Orleans, I didn't know so much of the city was really swamp, drained so humans could live here, a process that subsequently sank many neighborhoods below sea level. When P and I met during the first year I lived in Louisiana, I didn't know what to make of him: six-foot-six and, in some ways, too clean-looking for New Orleans back then, his skin untattooed, his brown hair cut short.

It was Halloween night, on a street corner crowded with dancing bodies, only blocks from the place we now live. I was twenty-two and he was twenty-three. We spoke briefly that night, and I continued to see him around. He often wore short jean cutoffs and loose, patterned, collared shirts with holes in them and, for Mardi Gras, tight-fitting dresses that accentuated his long, muscular legs. The way he held his large body was slightly effeminate. I watched his pronounced cheekbones, his big, mopey eyes, how he always sat with his legs crossed and put his hand over his mouth when he laughed. I didn't know then his distinct body language was that of a very tall person who was trying not to be seen. He was beautiful.

P's mom was nineteen when she had him and, when he was little, he spent many nights at his grandparents', a big house in the woods on the Northshore of Lake Pontchartrain. Before dinner they always said grace, and P would pray for a loophole to permit the dinosaurs—along with the 144,000 anointed human beings and billions of non-anointed ones—to be resurrected after Armageddon. His grandparents were young, as they also had his mom when they were in their late teens, so they were like a second set of parents to him; his grandmother had converted to the Jehovah's Witness faith when she was in her twenties. So P grew up knocking on doors. When I found this out a few months after we started hooking up, I wanted to understand how he broke free. I believed in Disney magic as a child—and, when I was in Catholic school, in the stories of the Bible as if they were fact—and P had grown up with the teachings of Jehovah's Witnesses, only to realize, a few years before he met me, that he wanted to try other ways to see the world. Something about P drew me out of myself; he was intelligent but not in the way I'd usually thought of intelligence—as something validated by prestigious gatekeepers. He made me question myself and the systems I'd accepted as normal growing up in New York City. He made me want to live another life.

Instead of working on James's film, I visit the shoot for a weekend. The drive down LA-1 to Grand Isle underscores the impossibility of this place:

a long bridge called "Gateway to the Gulf" from which you can see a patchwork of wetlands and the previous LA-1, a road now sinking into gulf. I stay with P, sleeping together on a sagging mattress in a beachside motel where the crew is staying. The motel, like all the buildings on Grand Isle, sits above the subsiding ground on stilts, and at night it sways in the wind. Intended for groups on summer fishing trips, the rooms are drafty, the walls and the bedding are thin, and it is so cold at night. Outside, there's the empty winter beach, at night the horizon lit up by shrimp boats and oil rigs. Quickly, I'm not sure why I came here. P is so busy and doesn't have time to hear me talk about my parents' new breakup or Jess or my hypothetical screenplay. My loneliness makes me miss him selfishly. Waking up every day long before sunrise, he paces around the motel with a tired, concerned look on his face, always on the phone convincing someone to be an unpaid extra in a bathing suit on the beach in winter.

I go to set for lunch and feel useless around all the people laughing together at something said over their walkies—earbuds stuffed in their ears, a conversation in their heads I'm not a part of. I watch James, a binder stuffed with papers under his arm and large headphones resting around his neck. He walks with the producers, having a very serious-faced conversation at a low volume, and he doesn't see me as I pass. I've never felt so much resentment seeing a friend do the work I thought I'd like to be doing, perhaps because it now seems so impossible for me to be doing it myself. I bring a slice of pizza back to P's motel room. I sit alone with the door open, letting in the cold air, and try to do some work on my laptop for the documentary director I'm doing research for. I'm distracted by the wind on the vacant beach, by the crew members who walk briskly past my open door, complaining to each other about someone, maybe James. *What's the difference between confidence and delusion?* I want to ask. I wish I could be confident/deluded. Perhaps then I could actually make something.

A friend, working in the art department on the film, asks if I'll pose in nude photos they need as props for the movie, and for some reason I comply—my tits out on the brisk winter beach and an awkward brown wig atop my shaved head while he takes the photos. I laugh uncomfortably at how ridiculous I must look, my hands tightly clasping a fishing rod I don't know how to use. The next day on set, I watch a guy I don't know pin the photo of my bare, pale skin and laughing face to the wall of the bar they're shooting in. I watch them set up the close-up shot, the male protagonist's point of view of the photo on the wall behind the bar, above dusty bottles of liquor. In the film he's meant to be staring at the photo intently, slightly confused, curious about the naked, fishing woman, wondering who she might be. I watch all those men gather around as they move the camera closer to the wall, focusing the lens on my frozen image. I too stare at myself within the frame. I look like a complete stranger.

the day after he tells me   every detail   plan b
i look up the girl he slept with: a,   i see her picture for the first time
and i touch myself   imagining p fucking her
is there something wrong with me?
i'm scared p will love someone more than he loves me
two days after it happens i imagine fucking a   without p   just me and her
the most empowering thing i can do is care
the most empowering thing i can do is not care
like beyonce, i'd rather be crazy
four days after it happens i send a one-sentence email to p:
"i realized why i'm so upset: i hate that you made me feel like a woman."

In the afternoon I walk on the beach and watch white birds move in coordinated patterns, scampering over sand then flying up over water, circling back to sand, moving in and out from the shore like waves. I sit on a rock and take my journal from my backpack. It's windy and cold and I don't write anything. Before I moved to Louisiana, I'd never seen a brown-water beach before, water dark with sediment, refusing to reflect the blue sky back to itself. Even here, on the coast, it's like swimming in the River.

Having met in college, my parents were around my age, late twenties, when they got married. It feels like an odd role reversal, him cheating on her, lying about it—my mom has always been the more outgoing, active-in-the-world parent—and I still find myself surprised my dad was capable of it, the lying part. My dad is a kind, funny man, and growing up, I was so happy to have a father who was not as recklessly self-assured or patriarchal as so many of my friends' fathers were. I've always been close with him. I've always been like him. Their first breakup lasted only a month or so before my dad moved back in with my mom mid-November, right after Trump was elected. At Thanksgiving we were all supposed to act like everything was normal again. Nothing was normal.

It's five and the sun is already setting and the shrimp boats are turning their lights on. One of the boats is fairly close to shore—I can see swarms of birds moving along with the vessel and frames hung with nets on either side of the boat like wings. I wander down the empty beach back to the motel, back to P's room. He's there but he's on the phone and, though his eyes move to me when I enter, he does not nod or otherwise acknowledge my presence. His phone is on speaker, and I can hear a man with a thick Cajun accent speaking loudly, perhaps with some anger, on the other end as P walks out the open door. Suddenly, I think again of summer, of A, of how she smells like flowers and dirt and sweat, of how this all started. I fall to the sagging mattress and cry quietly, attempting to stifle my breaths, so no one will hear me through the walls.

disneyfication

On a Wednesday night, we walk through the wet streets of the Bywater toward Montegut Street. The rain is cold, and P and I are scantily clad under thin, barely waterproof jackets. It's exactly a week before Ash Wednesday, so Mardi Gras is beginning to work toward its climax. We are headed to one of our favorite parties of the year.

Montegut Street is almost completely underwater. We cling to a chain-link fence as we move along the small strip of walkable sidewalk. A car full of fellow partygoers drives alongside us, gliding through the street like a boat, parting the murky water, its wake lapping toward us. Montegut is a quiet series of blocks, mainly warehouses and empty lots. Right now the only sign of life is the movement of barely clothed young people with glitter-covered faces locking their bikes and running through rain and dark puddles toward a squat warehouse in the middle of the block.

We follow them to a pop-up tent set up in an alley beside the building, one of those ubiquitous Louisiana tailgate and parade tents, a sign of commitment to outdoor events despite the constant intervention of the elements. Luckily, there's no line since we arrived early, around 10:00 p.m., so we gather under the small tent, where there's a table with two women taking money and marking the backs of hands with a thick Sharpie. Unlike most New Orleans parties, there's a cover. The price of entry is $15 at the door, and included with admission are five fake dollars given to you by the door girls, purple paper printed like money with the words: "Big Dick's House of Big Boobs." We are instructed to throw these dollars on the stage for our favorite acts, as the dancers will ultimately be able to exchange the purple currency for real money.

The Big Dick's DIY strip show used to happen several times a year, at various bars and warehouses around New Orleans, but it's been a year since the last one. Perhaps because the event had become infamous in the city and thus too crowded to continue without the knowledge of law enforcement. The organizers of this particular Big Dick's—the 2018 Mardi Gras incarnation of the party—have managed to keep the event relatively under wraps, no social media posts or flyers anymore, information on when and where spread primarily by word of mouth.

It's been three and a half weeks since the beginning of the strip club ban, and most of the city's strippers are still unable to work. As we enter the dark warehouse, I wonder if some of those unemployed women will be performing here tonight.

*

Meandering through hot, humid air from the riverfront, through my living room's open window, the eerie tinkling of the Steamboat Natchez's calliope makes its way to my ear. Three times a day, an older woman they call "Ms. Calliope" plays the steam-whistled instrument from the boat. When I hear the calliope later in the day, as the sun is going down, I think of my three friends—two are bartenders on the boat, and the other plays saxophone in the house band. Which of them is floating with all those tourists down the Mississippi tonight?

My first job in New Orleans was on Bourbon Street at Café Beignet, a Café Du Monde rip-off with an open courtyard and a live jazz band that, every day, played the same classic New Orleans–themed tunes such as "Walking to New Orleans" and "When the Saints Go Marching In." Our uniform was khaki pants and a shit-brown T-shirt that exclaimed, on the back, "Beignet, Done That!" Every morning at 6:30, I biked from my house near the fairgrounds down the stately tree-canopied Esplanade Avenue toward the Quarter. Once downtown I biked up Bourbon, which runs one way the opposite way but was relatively carless at that early hour. The sidewalks were usually empty save for a gutter-punk and her dog or a few super fucked-up tourists, stumbling toward their hotels on Canal Street. Often, my bike rides to work coincided with the street cleaners: noisy trucks that soak Bourbon Street with pungent cleaning fluid every single morning, only barely masking the stench of spilled beer and vomit and piss on hot pavement. The trucks push the mess of tangled, dirty beads from the street into the gutters, and people in neon shirts individually sweep up debris, every day fixing it up, preparing the street to be trashed all over again.

For a mere three nights, during the first few months I lived in New Orleans, my best friend/roommate and I held another job on Bourbon Street, just two storefronts down from Café Beignet but with very different hours. We sold "fishbowls" at Fais Deaux Deaux, a to-go bar attached to a strip club. Ashley and I started our shifts at Stiletto's around 7:00 p.m., walking through the strip club to access the bathroom-sized, street-facing bar area through a back door. The plastic fishbowls were sold for $10 a pop, $7 for refills, and contained a bright pink liquid consisting of fruit juice, grenadine, and "all the clear kinds of liquor," as Axe, the bartender who trained us, put it: bottom shelf rum, vodka, tequila, and Everclear. The fish bowl came with a neck strap, making the gigantic drink into a necklace, though Axe trained us to laboriously warn every customer that the strap was not equipped to hold the full fish bowl on its own. "Make sure to hold the bowl from the bottom," we cautioned each person, as if they were children. Some still turned around and immediately let go, spilling the contents of the drink on the entryway of the small space we inhabited those nights until around 4:00 a.m.

At Fais Deaux Deaux I witnessed, through the pinhole of the small bar's doorframe, the debauchery that preempted the morning clean-up. Hordes of people streamed past, so many of them forgetting how to walk, propped on the shoulder of a friend, careening down the street as if caught in fast-moving lava. One night Axe told us he never thought he'd end up working at a grown-up lemonade stand. "Don't drink on the job," he said with a wink and poured himself a shot. Once, I saw Axe pass a large bag of weed across the counter to a man with just a nod and realized why he kept the gig he hated so much.

Bachelor parties came in and asked us to change their bigger bills into stacks of ones and then headed next door to Stiletto's. They talked amongst themselves as if Ashley and I were invisible behind the bar; for the first time in my life I found myself privy to the way some men talk when women are not around.

At the end of our shift, after Ashley and I closed up the to-go bar, we reported to an all-night dive bar around the corner. There, we gave a guy behind the bar the cash from the drawer and our tips, and he went to the office in back to count. We waited at the bar with the patrons, men whose sweatshirts, jeans, and leathery faces were spray-painted silver or gold, men who were loosening up after being frozen all day—how strange it was to see these characters' natural movements as they brought bottles of beer to their lips, reminding me of a particular family story I've heard a thousand incarnations of. My mom was backstage at Disney, as a young girl, and saw Mickey with his fake head sitting on the picnic table beside him. His real head was wrinkled and hairless; he was smoking a cigar and spoke in a thick New Jersey accent. "Edna, how are ya?" he apparently coughed out to my great-grandmother, who had my mother, dressed for church, in tow. Soon, the guy would come from the back of the bar to give me and Ashley a very meager "training shift" portion of our tips.

After three nights of training, Ashley and I did not go back to Fais Deaux Deaux, though I continued to work on Bourbon, at Café Beignet, in the mornings. Working in the Quarter was repetitive and often gross, but there was a sense of community I enjoyed. I came to know the barkers on my block—I would flirt with the Stiletto's barker, whom I'd met when I'd sold fish bowls, as I walked by with my bike after getting off my shift at Café Beignet. Each day I saw the same little boys clacking down Bourbon, taps attached to their sneakers. I often ran into a few friends who pedi-cabbed and, sometimes, they gave me joyrides around the block. I recognized people I knew busking in bands around the Quarter, particularly my neighbor Allan, always wearing one of his handmade loincloths, playing his saxophone in Jackson Square. I saw people I knew and we smiled at each other, and I felt in those smiles that we understood something those folks we were surrounded by, holding their neon-colored drinks, would never understand.

In a way I loved being backstage to the large operation that is the New Orleans tourist industry. I also, however, had the privilege of knowing my stint there was impermanent; ultimately, I knew I wouldn't work on Bourbon for very long. I had my other world to fall back on—I had the freedom to make the decision that I didn't have what it took to observe daily that level of American excess and bodily fluids and still feign a smile for each rude customer that came in to order a "bag-nat," as they often mispronounced them. After a few months, I left Bourbon Street to bartend on Frenchmen and, later, to work at a hipster coffee shop in the Bywater. The people I worked with though, at Café Beignet and at Fais Deaux Deaux, had been working on Bourbon for years, being paid next to nothing, and yet maintained a level of customer service I could not imitate.

*

P and I buy cans of PBR at the bar, a surface of plywood haphazardly covered with cloth, before looking for an ideal place to stand near the center of the stage. The performance won't begin for another forty-five minutes or so, and the space is likely to get packed, providing a difficult viewing experience if you don't get a spot close enough to the action.

As we walk toward the front, I use my beer to chase swigs of whiskey from the small plastic Evan Williams flask carefully stored in my jacket pocket. The stage is maybe 35 feet long, a raised catwalk with a stripper pole installed at the front end, the top of the pole secured to structural metal beams of the warehouse ceiling. The origin of the catwalk branches out from a greenroom, concealed by a curtain that falls from a large arch, crafted from cloth and papier-mâché and built in the shape of a pair of wide-open, bent legs with heeled feet—the curtain is seemingly being birthed by a bright pink vagina between the prone legs. There's a handmade sign to the left of the stage, which looks like an iPhone and is glowing in the black light, that reads: "No Photos or Videos Ya Yuppie."

Big Dick's is an event that encourages shock value. The dances are meant to be sexy but, more importantly, they're meant to be weird, even disgusting, catering to unrealized fantasies. The acts invent new ways to understand the human body and all its secretions and orifices and ways of moving and, at the same time, make you laugh. The best acts repulse and seduce, eliciting gasps that come from both pleasure and disgust.

My first Big Dick's was over two years ago, and I thoroughly enjoyed myself, laughing and dancing and watching the acts with the forced attention of a very drunk person who's trying not to be. One of my favorite acts that night was a beautiful woman, mid-thirties, who danced onto the stage with several half-naked men holding a shower curtain around her. The curtain was opaque white, but occasionally a light would strike in the right way and her perfect nude silhouette would become visible and the crowd would shriek with delight. She was pregnant, very pregnant, and at first I thought this was probably an illusion, that she was likely wearing a fake belly behind the curtain. But then the men lowered the barrier, and she stepped out onto the stage, really naked and really pregnant. Her skin was covered in some kind of lubricant so her big belly and breasts were shiny, and she moved expertly around the stripper pole. I was surprised by how sexy she looked and then ashamed of my own surprise. Why had I not considered a pregnant body a sight capable of provoking arousal? Big Dick's makes you interrogate yourself, pointing an accusatory finger in your face and calling you judgmental, calling you a prude, and this is why I keep coming back for more.

*

The first time I ever came to New Orleans was on a road trip. I drove my parents' Honda Odyssey from New York to Louisiana with seven friends from college; we were sophomores and thrilled when we discovered Mardi Gras overlapped with our spring break, though admittedly I didn't really know what Mardi Gras was until I got to New Orleans. One of my friends had an older distant cousin in the city—when they got to talking, they couldn't figure out *how* exactly they were related—who we stayed with in his recently deceased mother's shotgun house in the Seventh Ward. The guests, all eight of us, squished onto two beds. During those two and a half days, we floated through the streets of New Orleans, and I fell in love with the city, its pulsing wildness. Only a few days before the road trip, a friend of mine had died, so I was lost and looking for meaning—New Orleans became the meaning. I knew I would be back.

I moved to New Orleans two years later, a few months after graduating from college. I met Ashley at a house party in New York, through another friend—she mentioned she'd also been interested in seeing what was up in New Orleans. Together, we drove south, and we soon discovered that not having a plan was quite normal in our new home; people in New Orleans never asked us why we'd moved here. We settled in quickly and became best friends.

By definition Manhattan is my home—I was born there and spent almost all my life there—and yet Manhattan cannot be contained or held by any one person, so it's never felt how I've imagined home to feel: like a possession, like a secret. I don't deserve ownership of New Orleans either, so I've restrained myself from getting a fleur-de-lis tattoo like so many misguided transplants before me (or, better yet, a stick-n-poke "Who Dat?" like the one I saw on a beautiful punk girl, the blurred words

of the Saints slogan resting incongruously below a tuft of armpit hair).
Yet New Orleans, unlike New York, has a tendency to feel intimate fast.
After only a few years here, I had become accustomed to the seasonal
repetitions of each year, the stupidly hot summers that lasted forever,
the busy, touristy winters, the energy and exhaustion of Mardi Gras.

My grandmother—Patty, who later married my grandpa Roy—was born
in New Orleans and lived here until she was only six, when her father
had to move to LA for work, but her family lived here for generations
before her. Those six young years loomed large in my familial imagination, as my grandmother always talked about this place and cooked
with too much butter. But she never moved back. I've often thought of
her; perhaps there's some kind of genetic lure that drew me into this
bowl of a city.

I didn't know what it meant to fall in love until New Orleans. In this city
I fell in love with Ashley, who made me realize who I wanted to be in
her joyful presence. We biked around New Orleans together, read books
under Spanish moss in City Park, went to dark dive bars during Saints
games to eat the free food the bartenders placed on plastic-covered pool
tables. We learned that on Sundays the sound of a brass band a few blocks
away signaled we should run to catch up with a Second Line parade. We
could walk along with the parade as far as it went, beer in hand, and let
the rest of the day wash away. We learned which restaurants had the
cheapest oyster happy hours and, on Ashley's birthday one year, we got
matching stick-n-pokes of very vaginal-looking oysters (I guess, admittedly, our version of a fleur-de-lis). Ashley had grown up in Harlem, only
subway stops away from my family's apartment on 86th, yet it was in
New Orleans that we came to know each other. Ashley: my best friend,
the one to pluck me out of the obscurity of being.

In this city I fell in love with P, who had grown up across Lake Pontchartrain from New Orleans in a family so different from mine, and yet who
seemed so familiar. We first kissed at a chaotic party, bathed in red light,

at the Dragon's Den during my first Mardi Gras living here. After that, we took drives over swamps on raised highways, speeding past tiny men in big pickup trucks, the flat, wet earth an intricate mystery beneath us. We took long walks through the Quarter, iced White Russians in hand, and ate messy po'boys as we sat on street corners. P taught me how to peel crawfish, tearing apart the delicate creatures to get at that miniscule yet satisfying chunk of meat, how to suck the salty juice from their torsos.

In New Orleans I came to know well each corner, each pothole that made my head rattle when I biked over it. I came to love the hot, stormy nights and my neighbors, an older couple, Nelson and Donna, across the street, sitting on their porch and singing along to Betty Wright playing fuzzily from an old boombox. I came to love the punk girls with their short-shorts and face tattoos, being dragged around the Bywater by their pit bulls. I fell in love with how our neighbors and people we met in bars and on the street were all impossibly friendly, even though Ashley and I were newcomers, even though we were so clueless. I fell in love with the way living here could somehow produce a level of happiness in me I didn't know was possible, but that happiness also couldn't keep the pain I felt here at bay—for me, New Orleans embodies this life on the precipice, existing in the in-between, inside of vulnerability, a place where one is constantly straddling joy and grief.

*

P and I pick out a spot to stand for the show, centered and at the end of the catwalk. Since P was born and raised in Louisiana and has lived in New Orleans longer, he often likes to wield his knowledge of this city and its culture over me like a distinguished degree. He was the first person to tell me about Big Dick's, and every time we go together now, he emphasizes how the show used to be far crazier in previous years, before it became so popular and overrun with New York transplants like me. He usually cites a particular night he went to Big Dick's before we'd met each other, and before I was cool enough to know about the event, when someone walked around the audience the whole night asking everyone who would comply to spit into a large jar. Toward the end of the night, the jar was supposedly brimming with spit, and since it was winter and everyone was coming down with something, there was a sufficient layer of yellow phlegm that had settled at the bottom of the container. During the final act of the show, a woman stripped down and, to the audience's horror, had the contents of their spit dumped all over her naked body.

In New Orleans, as in many urban areas in America, young people are always trying to prove their authenticity and, therefore, there's often this need to claim whatever came *before*, to insist on how it was superior to the present. A lot of this is posturing, a denial of the fact that by merely existing here, we are part of the problem—I know this, even as I participate. The warehouse we are in tonight, for example, is close to one of my first houses in New Orleans, in the Bywater, a largely Black neighborhood that, since Katrina, was declared "up-and-coming" and is rapidly being gentrified. When I lived in the Bywater, I thought often about the complicated state of being a transplant in New Orleans, a place I was deeply in love with yet where my presence was inherently problematic—a form of complicity if not an active role in what was happening to the neighborhood. When other transplants discussed crime, they often adopted the racist language used by native white New Orleanians to describe our block and the surrounding area: "the *other* side of St. Claude Ave.," "the dangerous side," "not that safe *yet*," or even "the ghetto side." These were the same people who longed for authenticity, who said things like *the Bywater was better when*. Yet, when it came to "crime," they were painting gentrification as a mode of eradicating something nefarious that had come before it.

When we first moved into that shotgun house in the Bywater several years ago, five white and Black kids in our early twenties, who'd all gone to college in the Northeast and were artists working in the service industry, we were the first of our kind on our block. None of us live there anymore, though the lease is still in our names, just with younger people, friends-of-friends living there in our place. Now, the street is all "fixed up" houses, the monthly $300 per room we were each paying largely unimaginable in that area, and our neighbors across the street have since been evicted. After they were kicked out, there was a dumpster outside their house for months. The landlord, the same owner as before, gutted the inside, as if the house were only worth restoring now that this was a neighborhood considered desirable by white people. I saw straight through that familiar house—the walls stripped to beams, the porch where Nelson and Donna would sit and sing together into the night, reduced to its parts—and at once understood gentrification could be truly violent. That it is a form of war.

Mardi Gras is a festival tinged with this contradiction for me: we are celebrating a place we are permanently altering the character of, a city we love but isn't really our home.

A little after 10:30 p.m., the emcee, a tall, skinny drag queen in very high heels and a Marie Antoinette wig, graces the stage with a mic and explains the rules. She tells us not to take pictures or videos while also encouraging our enthusiasm for the dancers. For as long as I can remember, the organizers have vehemently discouraged recording of the event—perhaps for fear of drawing unwanted attention from local authorities, who might catch sight of "lewd behavior" and large, unsanctioned crowds via social media—but this tradition also heightens a sense of exclusivity of what goes on inside these warehouse walls. If you miss a particular performance, even by simply going to wait in the long line for one of the porta potties outside, you will never be able to experience the excitement beyond your friends' retelling of what happened. (This is what happened to me once when two girls supposedly took turns peeing in each other's mouths.) You will always be left wanting to be among those who witnessed it for real.

A locally well-known DJ with a bald head and wisps of gray hair hanging from either side of his chin is on a raised part of the back of the stage behind his laptop, which sits on a plastic table surrounded by handles of alcohol. P's friend hands him a bag of molly, which P dips a spit-wet finger into and then offers to me. The sharp, acrid crumbs melt in my mouth as the emcee announces the first performer and the DJ cues up their song.

The first few acts are women who know their way around a pole. Perhaps they're professionals but taking risks they wouldn't be allowed to take at their day jobs on Bourbon Street. One woman gets very naked quickly, opens her legs wide as she leans against the pole just in front of us, and puts her fingers inside herself. I look at P, trying to ask with my eyes, *Is that allowed?* I can never seem to remember what's permitted here, or what happens when the border between performance and sex act has been breached. P shrugs and his nonchalance is the correct reaction— I've never seen an act halted for going too far. The woman crawls to the left side of the stage and starts flirting with a guy in the audience I used to bartend with a few years ago. He seems like he's into her though he doesn't appear to know her personally and also must be aware of all the eyes now fixated in his direction. He's smiling goofily as the woman squats in front of him, his head at crotch-level, and she gestures come-hither with her index finger. He puts his head between her thighs and the crowd whoops. When he moves his head back after a few moments, he's pulling a set of Mardi Gras beads, between his teeth, that he's retrieved from inside the dancer like a perverted sleight-of-hand trick.

Throughout the show, the emcee occasionally mentions the strip club ban and the subsequent unemployment of the city's strippers, well-known information met with boos from the audience. Starting on January 20th, the police began raiding and suspending the alcohol licenses of most of the strip clubs on and around Bourbon Street. The raids were performed supposedly in reaction to a suspicion the clubs were sites of human trafficking. However, the strippers who dance in these clubs adamantly refute this claim, saying they feel safe in their workplaces and have never witnessed such activity inside the clubs. During the raids, cops questioned and gathered IDs from women who were still in their stripping attire, basically naked, and allegedly forced the dancers to change in front of male officers. The cops yelled out legal names of strippers in front of customers despite the women's pleas not to do so. In the purported interest of helping women, of looking out for their safety, the city successfully put most dancers out of work right before the busiest season of the year, Mardi Gras, and right before the beginning of February, when rent would be due. Strippers marched down a busy Bourbon Street last Thursday night, through drunk crowds, with signs that read: "We are not victims," "The men who shut us down bought a dance last week," "This is NOLA, not Disneyland." The strippers also protested a news conference put on by New Orleans officials, which was meant to commemorate the opening of the "New Bourbon Street," a series of street renovations completed for the city's "tricentennial." The dancers drowned out speeches, chanting "Save our jobs!"[1]

The infrastructural upgrades made to Bourbon, such as the paving of potholes and the installation of bollards and security cameras, are viewed by the strippers and others in the city as undeniably linked to the raids. The current mayor, Mitch Landrieu, has been rumored to be courting Disney in the hopes of the company's creation of a major cruise ship port in New Orleans, which would be a serious boon for the city's tourist industry. Landrieu, therefore, has been working on "cleaning up" the Quarter, increasing security and ultimately aiming to shut down the strip clubs, not unlike former New York City mayor Giuliani's push to rezone and "Disneyfy" Times Square in the '90s. Giuliani succeeded in this venture, and the neighborhood once known for its strip clubs, porn shops, and peep shows is now an immense hub of family-friendly tourist attractions and blindingly bright billboards. Having grown up in New York City, I remember my parents speaking about the *old Times Square*, about how, when they first moved to New York in the '80s, 42nd Street was much "rougher," "seedier"—not unlike how I've more recently heard areas of New Orleans described. By the time I was in high school, Times Square was the site of a Toys R Us so large a Ferris wheel fit inside it. In high school my best friend and I would take the 1 train from the Upper West Side to Times Square and use our fake IDs to get gigantic margaritas at the absurdly crowded Dallas BBQ on 42nd. There, we ate crappy chili and corn bread, which I had nothing to compare to 'cause I'd never been to Texas—or anywhere, for that matter, near the South. We'd walk around Times Square and banter with guys who would speak in low, longing voices and seemed like drug dealers but were really just trying to get us to buy tickets for bad stand-up comedy shows. I loved walking through all the people on Broadway with purpose, even though I had nowhere to be, thrusting my body through throngs of clueless humans, people who would stop in the middle of the sidewalk and look up with a wonder at taking in the novelty of New York and its massiveness that I could never truly know. I would pretend Times Square was a mosh pit, pushing and weaving through strangers in my Doc Martens, not giving a shit, because this was the only way I felt I could claim the city as mine—with the certainty of my stride, the confidence of my movement.

I was in college when the Disney store opened in Times Square. That summer I went down to 42nd Street, alone, to repeat my mosh-pit ritual. I saw the huge storefront for the first time, that gleeful incarnation of capitalism with my other, secret last name emblazoned in bright lights across the exterior, and felt like such a fraud. I went inside the store that night and rode the endless escalator. I walked aimlessly through the crowded space, through aisles and aisles of memorabilia, plastic and plush figures that seemed to scream at me through forced smiles; I wasn't walking with my New Yorker confidence anymore. I felt separate from the body I was inside of, reminding myself this place was somehow a part of me.

Now, I wonder if Bourbon Street will experience the same evolution, the same kind of death, as Times Square, at the expense of these women and their livelihoods, because of something created long ago by a man I am related to. I'm sure it will be more than just the French Quarter—it's already happening. How will the whole city of New Orleans find itself altered?

Later in the night, two men get on stage, one dressed as Forrest Gump and the other sitting on his legs in a wheelchair, Lieutenant Dan. The two guys make out, Forrest Gump intermittently straddling Lieutenant Dan and dancing around him. Eventually, Lieutenant Dan leaps from his wheelchair and they dance together, undressing completely, each ultimately bending over to receive a butt plug inserted by his partner. Attached to the butt plugs are short strings with several real grilled shrimp attached to them, which the guys swing from their asses in circles above a captivated audience.

*

In the past few years, Disneyland has faced controversy over the company's treatment of workers, paying minimum wage, forcing their "cast members" to live paycheck to paycheck (while, of course, continuing to train them to always smile). Rising housing costs in Anaheim have made it increasingly difficult for Disney employees to find affordable housing near the park. Many have long commutes from other cities, while others live in long-term motels or even out of their cars. Disneyland is the largest employer in Anaheim and is also a primary cause of the city's unprecedented houseless crisis, with almost 4,800 people experiencing houselessness on any given night. A 2018 report published in the Los Angeles Times found that 85 percent of Disneyland workers are paid less than $15 an hour. "Workers at the Anaheim resort are paid so little that more than 1 in 10 report being homeless at some point in the last two years, two-thirds say they don't have enough food to eat three meals a day and three-quarters say they can't afford basic expenses every month."[2] In November 2016 a sixty-one-year-old woman named Yeweinishet Mesfin—an immigrant from Eritrea who worked as a custodian in Disneyland—was found dead in her car a few days after a missing person's report was filed.

Meanwhile, Disney CEO Bob Iger was paid $65.7 million in 2018, 1,000 times the median salary of Disney employees.[3] In recent years the company has continued to expand, becoming the most powerful studio, seemingly consuming everything in its path. Disney paid $4 billion apiece for the Marvel and Lucasfilm empires, around $10.5 billion for full control over Hulu and, in 2019, the company acquired Fox for a baffling $71.3 billion.[4]

In summer 2018 my sister went with my mom to speak to a group of Disneyland employees at the union in Anaheim. Recently, my sister recounted the meeting to me, where they heard firsthand from the workers about their experiences and how, through their stories, she came to realize the intensely manipulative nature of Disney's maltreatment. A younger woman in her late twenties, who worked as a janitor at the park, talked about how they didn't get healthcare coverage and, apparently, the new *Frozen*-themed attraction had rampant black mold inside it that was making workers sick. She said she was paid $11 an hour and, at the local public school, she could've been paid $18 an hour, but she loved working at Disney—or the idea of it—since it was a special place that had meant so much to her as a kid. My sister told me, "I have a vague memory of her saying she worked at night, and I remember picturing her, mopping or sweeping while the park was empty, thinking that must've felt sort of special in a way, to get to be there while it was empty, to feel like a caretaker for a place that you love."

A very slim woman in her fifties, who worked in the costume department, told them that over the thirty years she had worked for Disney, her pay had only slightly increased and she'd never been promoted to a managerial position. Other workers in the group echoed that managers were rarely promoted from within, and instead were hired and brought in from the outside. With former restaurant managers coming in, people who'd never actually worked the job performed by those they were overseeing, an obvious tension was cultivated between the two groups. My sister said this seemed like a deliberate strategy on Disney's part to prevent solidarity building between workers and managers, as she doubted that managers were being treated very well either.

Another woman they met, a middle-aged concierge at a hotel, who my sister said was clearly a "Disney superfan," had a particularly hard time describing the exploitive nature of the job. She talked about not being able to afford her rent, since this was the purpose of the meeting, but it was clear she'd rather talk to my mom and sister about everything she loved about Disney and her job. My sister recounted, "It was upsetting to see that split, to see how even this person who loved Disney so much, who seemed so attached to and invested in the fun, happy fantasy world it created, couldn't ignore as much as she wanted to the painful reality that working there was creating in her life."

One of the reasons Disney can keep workers, despite the poor treatment, is because of the unique allure of the job. In an article published by the *Guardian* about protests of Disneyland's low wages, an employee reiterates that they love their jobs at Disney—they just want to be paid a living wage.[5] Many of these employees want jobs at Disney *because* it's Disney, because they watched the films growing up, because they went to the park as a kid and wanted to believe in the power of imagination. And, of course, Disney knows this, as they were the ones who made the imagination into something marketable.

*

During intermission, a well-known New Orleans rapper, a young, bald-headed woman wearing her classic black tank top, "Goddess" tattooed in large letters across her chest, takes the stage and stuns us all with her powerful voice. She screams her rhymes into the mic, and she kills it.

Later, my former next-door neighbor Allan performs. He's falling over himself as he dances, pulling off his clothes in an unmethodical manner and holding desperately onto the metal pole to swing himself in circles around it and also perhaps because he needs it for support. Since, in the light of day, Allan exclusively wears loincloths, seeing him in a state of undress is nothing out of the ordinary. Despite his apparent inebriation, he manages to move with athleticism up the pole toward the ceiling with bizarre determination. When I talk to him later in the night, his eyes are sleepy and he speaks slowly, saying he remembers nothing of his dance until he found himself suspended by his knees from one of the metal beams on the ceiling—he'd climbed all the way up the stripper pole and launched his legs up there, but he has no memory of this.

Fatal Rhododendron is one of the last acts, and they are stunning, wildly swinging the tresses of their long hair while twerking, and doing some very experienced pole tricks, thanks to their impressively toned leg and arm muscles. Their Instagram bio reads, *Divine feminine meets masculine*. At Big Dick's, Fatal Rhododendron is royalty, and they do not disappoint.

*

P and I live in the French Quarter now, just a block into the "Lower Quarter," the quieter side of the neighborhood, where Bourbon becomes a residential street. Groups of tourists still walk down it until the street dead-ends, leaving them confused and lost in a nearby area known as the Marigny triangle. We hear them from the apartment as they continue down Bourbon, crossing the intersection, their loud, inebriated voices momentarily echoing off the two-story houses that line our street.

Living in the Quarter is sometimes like living in a fucked-up museum or amusement park. Horse-drawn carriages click down our street, while Segway tours quietly speed past. Tour guides speak over microphones about the architecture, and tourists take photos of the houses on our block, which oddly reminds me of when I was ten and we lived for several years on Central Park West—when the big red sightseeing buses were paused at the light at our corner, I could hear someone on a microphone incorrectly exclaiming "Walt Disney's kids live there," pointing to our house.

Verti Marte, the closest corner store to our current apartment, is on the same intersection as the "most haunted house in New Orleans," the LaLaurie Mansion, once inexplicably owned by Nicolas Cage and a popular stop for ghost tours. Sometimes, I leave the store with a bag of chips or a roll of toilet paper and try to ignore the theatrics of the tour guides across the street. It's not uncommon for three large tour groups to be crowded at the intersection, each guide shouting to their group about the grisly torture Madame LaLaurie inflicted on the enslaved people who lived there. Her harsh behavior was suspected by the neighborhood because "her slaves were known to be on edge," the tour guides say, but the extent of her cruelty was not known until the mansion caught fire. The neighbors rushed in to help LaLaurie save her valuables, finding the enslaved people starving, tortured, and chained up in the attic. The sensationalism of this tale and how it begs to overshadow the horrific day-to-day reality of slavery is made more disquieting by the wide variety of the tour guides' narratives—how they yell over each other in front of the mansion, how they seem to be competing to tell the most graphic, disturbing version of the story.

*

I don't see Roxanne or Sarah here tonight, the two strippers I know who've been put out of work by the raids, perhaps because of Big Dick's steep price of entry. The last time I saw Roxanne was a little over a week ago at our friend Lizzie's birthday party at a karaoke bar. Roxanne told me about the raids, and how she had only $30 to last her through the week. I was buying her drinks, and she was getting wasted and ended up lying on the sticky floor of the bar and doing a sexy-drunk-lying-down dance while Lizzie sang Fleetwood Mac. I'd bought her drinks because it had seemed to be a way to support her in the moment, but then I was kicking myself for contributing to her demise, for not offering a more productive or compassionate form of care.

Lizzie and Roxanne are a few years younger than me and are best friends, from the suburbs of Portland, and live together in a shotgun house on my old street in the Bywater. Lizzie is very tall with long, hairy legs and a thick gauged ring through her septum, and Roxanne is a petite, delicate-looking girl with a black bob. Roxanne has given Lizzie a lot of her tattoos, including my favorite: a stick-n-poke of a cockroach climbing up Lizzie's calf. The story goes that one morning, just after stumbling out of bed, Lizzie felt an itch move across the skin of her lower leg, then looked down to find a fat New Orleans cockroach circumventing the round of her knee. She flicked the creature off, stomped it with a nearby shoe and, that night, asked Roxanne to give her a stick-n-poke in the bug's likeness. Roxanne drives a grumbling old blue Buick, and the floor of her bedroom is littered with vinyl platform boots. She's been in the industry for five years, she tells me at Lizzie's birthday. She likes dancing because it's lucrative, because she makes her own schedule, and because it's reliable. She talks about women she knows who pay for school and others who pay for their kids' schooling with money from stripping. A year or so ago, Roxanne was fired from Barely Legal because she put her finger in a guy's mouth while giving him a lap dance—or she put *his* finger in *her* mouth, she can't remember. Now she dances at Rick's Cabaret, one of the many clubs targeted by the raids.

Some strippers say tourists on Bourbon Street, showing their boobs for beads, get away with more than what is deemed legal behavior for the professionals at strip clubs in the Quarter. During the Mardi Gras strip club raids and the aftermath, no arrests would be made for human trafficking. Some clubs, however, were cited for their strippers' "lewd, immoral, or improper entertainment," which can mean exposing one's breasts or buttocks anywhere in the club other than the raised stage, or simulating sexual acts or masturbation, including touching one's own breasts while dancing. At the protests the strippers talked about the city's "tricentennial"—itself an imagined concept, as if this place, formerly called by the Choctaw name Bulbancha, "land of many tongues," where forty distinct Native groups met, traded, and fished, only truly came to exist when it was claimed by the French and dubbed

"La Nouvelle-Orléans"—and how sex work has been one of this place's foremost industries for three hundred years.

*

In his imagining of the Disney parks, Walt was supposedly inspired by the city of New Orleans. Disneyland's "New Orleans Square" was the first new "land" to be built after the park's opening in 1955, dedicated in 1966 with Walt and the current mayor of the city, Victor H. Schiro, in attendance.[6] The New Orleans Square, which contains a mini–French Quarter street and restaurants, Creole Café and Blue Bayou, was Walt's last major project as he died only a few months after the dedication.

According to legend, Walt's discovery of a mechanical bird in a New Orleans antique shop was the primary inspiration for the animatronic characters now so ubiquitous in the parks. After purchasing the bird, he brought it back to the imagineers at his California studios, asking them to try to improve the antique's mechanics and find a way to make the bird's beak move on cue to music or speech. The imagineers succeeded, creating the technology for what Walt called "Audio-Animatronics." In the original planning for Disneyland, Walt sent one of his top imagineers, Harper Goff, to New Orleans to observe Mardi Gras traditions.[7] It's likely Walt's love of New Orleans is the reason parades are so central to the experience of both Disneyland and Disney World.

Another myth purports that Walt once considered the now wildlife refuge Bayou Savauge, wetlands across Lake Pontchartrain from New Orleans, right where P grew up, as a possible location for Disney World. Instead, the company purchased acres of swampland in Florida; like New Orleans, whose "tricentennial" marked three hundred years of forcing permanence atop a landscape meant to be always changing, Disney World celebrates the human desire to subjugate nature.

Having heard all these stories and myths about his love of this city, I am surprised to find that Walt's first introduction to New Orleans was in scouting and researching for *Song of the South*. How strange it is to now live in an apartment from which I can hear, at least once a week, the Steamboat Natchez's calliope playing that familiar tune from the film: *Zip-a-dee-do-dah, Zip-a-dee-ay* . . .

*

Disneyfy—the word reminds me of *gentrify* and, in New Orleans, I'm not really sure there's a difference. They're at least cogs in the same machine. It's been over a year since the Mardi Gras strip club raids, and now it's confirmed that the Disney Cruise Line is coming to New Orleans. The cruise ship terminal where the Disney ships will dock is rumored to be in the process of construction near the levee in the Bywater called the "End of the World." The Disney Cruise website reads: "Be among the first to set sail with Disney Cruise Line from New Orleans—a unique port city that is hip, contemporary and yet seemingly untouched by time. Departures begin during the Mardi Gras season, which kicks off with weeks of colorful festivities culminating on 'Fat Tuesday.'"

The Dictionary.com definition of *Disneyfy* is "to create or alter in a simplified, sentimentalized, or contrived form or manner." To Disneyfy, then, is to suppress or deny reality.

*

Around 3:30 a.m. the final few acts of Big Dick's perform to a very wasted and rowdy crowd. Most of the audience is now dancing along to the music, many are facing away from the stage, forgetting the performers, and some are passionately pressing their tongues against those of their newfound partners. I'm sure these performances are just as energetic and imaginative as the first ones, but they are unlikely to be as memorable due to the state of the audience.

Around 4:00 a.m. the dancers stop coming out and the event devolves into a large dance party, members of the audience jumping up onto the catwalk to dance, pretending to be as brave as the performers they've watched throughout the night. I see a friend of mine hanging drunkenly from the stripper pole and haul myself up onto the stage next to her. I'm wearing a hot pink fishnet dress I bought at an exotic dancewear store on Haight Street when I last visited Nonna in San Francisco, where she's lived all ninety-one years of her life. I bought the dress with Mardi Gras in mind. Part of the dress covers my nipples but, when I dance, the fabric moves around, and several times while I'm teetering up there on the catwalk, I realize my boobs are completely visible and that they've turned on the overhead lights in the warehouse. But then I remember that everyone is wasted and no one is looking at me. Most of the people I'm dancing with are as naked as, if not more than, I am.

The performers from tonight are celebrities dancing among us, their bodies known, famous, to us now. I wonder if Roxanne has ever considered performing at Big Dick's, in this space where she could bring every weird, funny part of herself to the dance, where she could be seen as the artist her friends know her to be. How long will the strip club ban last; how long will she and others be jobless? Will Landrieu succeed in undermining the strip clubs and these women, who dance not to be seen, like at Big Dick's, but to simply live?

*

The week after Big Dick's, on Fat Tuesday, P and I wake up late, at 7:30. We rush to put on our outfits. I stretch a mesh dress over my body, then tape the King Cake Baby pasties I made the day before to my nipples. Over his bare chest, P wears a purple jacket; on the back, our friend has sewed in sequin cursive "Tall Baby." P and I cover our faces in Vaseline, carefully dabbing glitter on so it will hold. We bike to the End of the World, a grassy spot at the end of the Upper 9th Ward levee, beyond the train tracks and the abandoned Naval facility, where the Industrial Canal meets the Mississippi River. A group of our friends is already there, Ashley and others, vibrantly costumed and grinning, some of them cleaning the shrooms from their teeth by swishing mouthfuls of

Gingeroo from a shared bottle. Someone has driven four wooden posts into the muddy earth, creating a square sort of altar, and hanging from the posts are many colorful scraps of fabric, tossing violently in the wind. It's a sunny, unseasonably warm day, the light constantly changing because the clouds are moving so fast in front of the sun. Steamboats and barges lazily float down the Mississippi; some blow their horns as they round the sharp turn. Perhaps they're honking at us. What is it like to drive a steamboat, and to drive it past New Orleans on Mardi Gras day?

Our friends Joan and Jesse are getting married. They've lugged a PA system out to the levee, and some friends play music and sing as Joan and Jesse approach us, hand in hand. Jesse is wearing a fencing mask he's covered in mirror shards, a helmet of differently angled reflections, blue-painted chopsticks dangling like a beard from the bottom. Joan has on a tall, bedazzled headdress and a gown made of multicolored ribbons over a black bathing suit. Another friend, Nathan, was ordained to perform the ceremony. He guides the ritual in a manner not so different from how he directs his experimental plays. When the time comes, Joan digs through Jesse's fanny pack and pulls out the rings.

After the vows the band plays a few songs and P allows for a rare cheesy activity, maybe 'cause of the mushrooms, and we slow dance together to their rendition of "Sea of Love." I reach my arms up around his big, sequined shoulders, and he hunches over so his face can be closer to mine. We sway slowly to the music and kiss, our sticky, glittered noses pressing toward each other. It's been exactly four years since my lips met his for the first time. *Happy Mardi Grasversary*, he says, but a friend pushes the lens of his film camera into our faces, definitively ruining the moment.

After the band finishes playing, we make our way, as a group, down the levee, back over the train tracks into the Bywater. Hundreds of people are gathered on Burgundy Street with costumes more elaborate than any of ours. Soon, what felt like our large parade of wedding-goers is subsumed by the true parade. For the rest of the day, we walk with St. Anne's through the Marigny and the French Quarter, gathering more and more people along the way, snaking through hordes of tourists who then join us, until it seems as if the whole city has become a part of the parade. The streets transform into a stage everyone can perform on, which takes some of the pressure off the more fearful of us who, for once, join along. P and I continue to lose and find Ashley and our other friends, occasionally stopping at bars, making our way to what we know to be the end point of St. Anne's: a spot on the Moon Walk, upriver from where we started our day.

We arrive in the afternoon, the parade having thinned quite a bit since it moved out of the more populated part of the Quarter. The brass band plays "Down by the Riverside" and advances toward the rocks that slope down at the bank of the River. P and I find a big boulder, sitting at a slight distance from those at the front of the parade, who walk down to the edge of the River to dump Ziploc bags and Domino sugar boxes full of their loved ones' ashes into the water. The parade leaders take the tall, ribbon-covered poles they've been carrying for the length of the parade and dip them into the River, flinging water on us and the others gathered on the rocks.

We watch this mournful scene, droplets of water and the ashes of strangers who died in the past year carried on the wind to where we are sitting. A man in a skin-tight tiger costume and full tiger-face makeup runs down the rocks beside us, tripping and falling right at the edge of the bank. He accidently drops—almost throws—an open plastic bag of dried flowers and ashes into the River. His arm hovers over the spot where the bag slipped from his grasp, and we watch as the ashes disappear into murky water. Soon, his shock fading, he sighs and picks himself up off the rocks. Then, laughing sadly to himself at his own clumsiness, he turns to P and me, the few who witnessed his fall: *Well, I guess that's one way to do it.*

Perched on an uncomfortable rock, leaning against P, I allow the cold droplets of the River to land on my face without wiping them away. I forget everything except for my love for this city, for P—sometimes they are the same feeling. Stretched between P and me, binding us together, is New Orleans, a place where you can inhabit the imagination, where you can attend a wedding and a funeral on the same day as if it's a continuation of the same celebration. How wonderful it is to spend a day this way, to just walk and walk, until walking feels like dancing, to the River.

grand isle part II

A barrier island is barely a place, an accident of tidal movements. An edge, a slippage. I sit up on the bed in the cold motel room in Grand Isle, wondering what I should do with myself. It's dark out now, but they're probably still shooting. From the bed, I can see out the window to the gravel parking lot—a P.A. walks briskly across the lot with his arms straining around stacked pallets of plastic water bottles. A costumer who looks and dresses like an old movie star is leaning against a car, forlornly smoking a cigarette. In the next room, the producer's assistant is on the phone. She's gossiping loudly and stomping around her bedroom. She must be looking for something, rummaging. From what I can hear, she's apparently sleeping with a grip and electric guy. She erupts in laughter at whatever is being said on the other line. I stare at the motionless, dusty ceiling fan. I write a film in my head.

EXT./INT. FRENCH QUARTER COFFEE SHOP—
NEW ORLEANS—AFTERNOON

It's a mild, slightly windy day for the usually oppressive New Orleans summer and so the coffee shop is fairly busy. Locals with dogs and face tattoos sit at the tables outside. Tourists in matching "Drunk 1" and "Drunk 2" shirts lumber around in groups, out-of-season Mardi Gras beads clicking incessantly around their necks.

P (late 20s), a very tall guy in jean cut-offs and a ratty floral shirt, and I (late 20s), a girl-person with a shaved head and a centered lip ring hugging her bottom lip, who somehow doesn't look as punk as that sounds, sit at a small table inside with sweating glasses of iced White Russians. Our bodies are now unsure how to relate to each other's in public, my eyes still uncertain how to meet his. P's long legs are crossed, his torso angled slightly away from me.

We've met up to have another *talk*. For the past week, our talks have consisted of a looped conversation, the same angry criticisms and hopeless apologies over and over again, until we go somewhere to fuck.

I pull from my backpack my amputated ponytail and place it on the table between us like Van Gogh's ear.

ME
(*smiling*)
I saved this for you—it's four years, like us.

P
(*laughing*)
You're absurd . . .
You know, I loved your shaved
head, when we first met—

ME
You hated it! You said
you couldn't introduce me to your family!

P
(*laughing, covering his mouth with his hand*)
I was joking, you know I was.

We're silent for a few beats and suddenly I notice: P's eyes, they're watering. I sip my White Russian through a straw, regarding this unfamiliar P with curiosity.

ME
I think I still need more time.

                                P

                    (laughing, wiping his eyes but
                 otherwise not acknowledging his tears)
                            Yeah, yeah...
                    It's weird but, as much as this sucks,
                        I kind of like you like this...
               You seem more confident, like at the beginning.

                               ME

                            (laughing)
             So you only like me when I'm breaking up with you?

                                P

                            Maybe.

I lean across the table and kiss him. Maybe I do too. I've been scared
for a long time, I realize. I'm scared I don't know how to be a woman
in love with a man without losing a part of myself. I'm scared the
part of myself I'll lose is the part I like best—the fighting part, the
part that knows they're already whole.

I pull away, finding my way back into my seat, his dark eyes holding mine.

                                P

                 She still wants to meet you, if you do.
                     I mean, without me there.

                               ME

                            (sighing)
                        I'll think about it.

But, really, I already know what I'm going to do.

After my parents broke up the first time, I told P I wanted to turn our
monogamous relationship into an open one, like a magic trick. I didn't
want what my parents had—I wanted the truth, I thought I could find it

somehow, I thought it was possible to anticipate the hurt. I didn't know how jealousy finds so many different ways to whisper to you. Though I told him I wasn't sure how we were going to enact it, P was okay with the idea. Because he was raised by people who loved him dearly yet wholeheartedly believed the world might end at any moment, P viewed most social institutions as absurd and limiting. He didn't believe in national anthems or birthdays or romance or marriage. Sometimes this denial of the expected could be unbelievably frustrating, like how he'd never given me a card or planned a party for me or surprised me. But it also played into our connection, because I could be frustrating in the same way, groaning about the sexist constraints of relationship expectations, of romance. Even though P could be cynical, even harsh in his delivery—my friends often thought he was an asshole when they first met him—I liked so much that he was honest. And I could tell him anything. We were partners in this experiment, attempting to find out if there was a different way to be together, a way that felt a little like falling apart.

The producer's assistant is laughing again, and I feel weird about how clearly I can hear her through the wall. I walk outside, onto the porch, into the cold night air rolling off the Gulf.

P told me about A on the phone while I was out of town this past summer, a girl he'd met recently and was interested in, a gardener in Baton Rouge. He said I might like her too; he thought she might want to have a threesome with us. I didn't know her, I'd never had a threesome and, secretly, it scared me, but it was funny to talk about. That week she cut his hair in her apartment, her hands moving over his scalp. A few days later, the night before I came back to New Orleans, they slept together.

I walk down the wooden stairs, into the gravel parking lot. The babely costumer is no longer outside smoking, and the parking lot is empty. I make my way to the main road, the only street that runs the length of the skinny island of Grand Isle. There aren't many streetlights and it's dark and I walk along the shoulder, massive pickup trucks careening a little too fast and too close to me. They're filming at a dive bar up the road. In the distance I can see the big movie lights and huge equipment trucks, obscuring my view of the squat one-story bar.

When I got back to New Orleans that summer night, I asked P to stay at a friend's place for a week or so. Immediately sharing a bed with him seemed like defeat. I was angry at the part of myself who thought he wouldn't be able to do it, like I hadn't. Since we'd decided to be open, I'd kissed other people and there were a few instances when I could've slept with someone else—they were men, the ones who sex seemed possible with—but then I always remembered how strange sleeping with men could be, the dangerous unpredictability of them, how the ordeal was often not satisfying beyond the story. I arrived home with my hair well past my shoulders and a restlessness I could cure only by asking Ashley to help me shave my head again. I sat on a milk crate in our apartment as Ashley took the base of my thick ponytail in her small hand and worked through four years of hair with a pair of scissors. I felt the clippers warming against my scalp and remembered—the last time I shaved my head was on a hot September night, just hours before I told P I loved him for the first time. I said it as he drove us across Lake Pontchartrain over the causeway ("the longest bridge she'd ever crossed," sang Lucinda Williams) and thought by the time we finally got off that bridge, onto land, maybe I would change my mind. But I didn't.

There's a gigantic puddle, and I wait for a car to pass so I can walk around it, so I can remember there's still hard ground to stand on, even as this island sinks into the Gulf. Outside the dive bar, guys with tool belts are jumping in and out of trucks with engines running and standing around smoking cigarettes and not looking at me with such purpose I feel like someone playing a ghost in a movie. The main door to the bar is blocked by a huge light, so I walk to the back, where I wait at the door until a PA standing nearby yells "cut" at no one in particular, and I sneak in.

It's too easy to look away from the truth when it scares us. We say, *My boyfriend fucked another girl and I don't want to know what she looks like, how he touched her, I don't want to know how her skin felt under his.* But not knowing doesn't negate what happened. Even if you don't look at her, she will still have a beautiful face. It's like the choice of the horror filmmaker to not show you the severed head inside the box. Instead, you are shown the outside of a box and told that there's a severed head in there and you scream. Our imaginations are more powerful, more terrifying, than any amount of SFX. This is, at least, what I told myself as I biked in the insanely hot, humid afternoon air toward the bar in the Marigny where A and I had agreed, over text, to meet for the first time. It began to rain lightly as I pedaled down Esplanade Avenue that day, the drops mingling with sweat on my stubbly scalp as my wheels fought with craterous potholes, so many of them as I got closer and closer to the Marigny. When I got there, it was a little after 4:00 p.m. and A was sitting at the bar, hunched over a book, her back to the door. I couldn't see her face, but I knew it was her because she was wearing her hair in two short braids like in the pictures I'd seen of her on Instagram. *Life is weird*, a silly sentiment I said to myself, taking a breath, my last chance to run away. Instead, I walked up to her. And she was beautiful, a smile spreading wildly across her face when I said her name. She pulled me into a hug and I smelled her, flowers and dirt and sweat. I complimented her cute, messy bangs and she told me she cut them herself. She was charming, bashful. She bought us beers and shots of whiskey, both of us laughing at the idea of our "mutual friend" and the fact we were dressed almost identically in worn yellow T-shirts cut with scissors into crop-tops, faded black jeans cut into shorts. For a few hours, we talked, laughed, got day-drunk. On the street outside the bar, both of us leaning against her Toyota Tacoma, the same model I used to own, I could feel her lingering, as if she didn't want to drive home, so I kissed her. She kissed me back. My arm on the edge of the truck's bed, I pressed my body toward hers and felt like a cowboy.

Inside, the bar is unbearably warm from bright lights and bodies and smells of sweat and fake smoke from the smoke machine. I see my friend James directing, and admittedly he's wearing it well. I watch him with fondness, thinking of when he got his nose kicked in at a punk show in college—how many characters he's been, we've all been. He gestures energetically with his hands as he talks quietly to the lead actor, who's sitting on a barstool. The lead actress is sitting at another stool down the bar as a makeup artist pats her face with a sponge. P is in a corner next to the cigarette machine with the background actors, who are leaning over, filling out paperwork on the pool table. He sees me and smiles slightly, perhaps surprised I'm on set.

INT. BEDROOM—NEW ORLEANS—MORNING

A girl (mid 20s) with messy brown hair and bangs is lying in bed, sleeping, beside me. I am awake, looking at sleeping A, the girl P had sex with only weeks earlier—now, bizarrely, filling the spot in bed usually occupied by P. Despite the implications of the circumstances, however, A and I are both fully clothed.

I tentatively reach out to put my hand on A's face, my fingers hovering over skin—I'm nervous. But then my phone buzzes loudly. I pull my hand back, turning over to find my phone on the floor. It's a message from P: "What happened???"

I type a response: "Nothing." But I don't send it, remembering the painful not-knowing I felt when P spent the night with A. I might as well tease it out a little longer.

A rustles beside me and I turn back toward her. She opens her eyes slowly and smiles. When she speaks, she reveals a slight Southern accent.

                                          A

                              Mornin'...

Still lying down, A stretches her arms above her head and yawns deeply.

ME

Hey, mornin'.

I throw my phone back to the carpeted floor.

A

God, I'm so fucking thirsty.

ME

Here...

I reach over to the bedside table and grab a plastic cup of water,
handing it to A, who pushes herself upright to drink. A chugs the rest
of the water in the cup, some of it dripping onto her tank top in her
haste. I laugh.

A

I need more!

A clumsily jumps out of bed and stumbles into the kitchen, fills the
cup to the brim, and chugs it at the sink. When she's done, she fills
it again and brings the cup back to the bedroom. She sits back down
next to me on the bed.

A

(*laughing, slightly embarrassed*)
Sorry. I guess I'm hungover—
I don't know how to handle hangovers anymore.

ME

(*smiling*)
Same.

A hands me the plastic cup. I drink from it and place it on the bedside
table, turning back to A. For a few beats, we silently look each other
in the eyes. I hold A's gaze purposefully, while she looks back at me
somewhat timidly. The moment possesses an intensity I know I have
to grasp in my hands before it's too late, before A leaves, and I will

remember this night as a strange sleepover, and we will be nothing more than new friends, friends who've had sex with the same guy, who happens to be my partner.

I move toward her, I hold A's face in my hand and put my lips to hers. A kisses me back, first tentatively, then more forcefully. I move my hand down the side of A's torso to her lower back, pulling her closer. We kiss until she pulls back slightly, smiling. I take my hands back nervously. We laugh, looking down but then at each other, sweetly, until—

                              A
                       (*smiling still*)
                       I should go.

                             ME
              Oh, okay. You have to drive back
                     to Baton Rouge?

                              A
                 Yea, I gotta work today.
                    I'm already late.

                             ME
                    Shit, I'm sorry.

A stands up and gathers her fanny pack and boots from a corner of the room. She sits on the bed, not facing me, to put on her shoes.

                              A
               We should hang out again.

                             ME
                    Yea, for sure...

INT./EXT. FRONT DOOR—NEW ORLEANS—MORNING

I hold the front door open, watching A get into her pickup truck, parked on the street in front of my house. A turns the key, and the old car groans loudly. A cranks the manual window down to yell over the engine at me.

A

See you soon! Thanks for saving me from
drunk driving back to Baton Rouge last night.

M E

Of course!

A puts the car in gear and drives away, down the street, turning a corner and out of view. I walk back to my bedroom, pick my phone up from the floor. There are five messages from P. The last one: "Gahh … you're killing me here. I guess you're probably fucking her."

The scene is not exactly the way it went down, but it's close. It's the movie version, more concise than the truth. Though, in the act of imagining it, it's as if I've made the scene real; perhaps this *is* what happened, or how I will remember it now. There were a few other times when A and I met up and we kissed—I always kissed her first—then someone pulled away, I was never sure who, and she had to go. We talked for hours before I got the courage to kiss her. We talked and talked even after a kiss had passed and I couldn't bear to try again. No one would have the patience to watch those scenes. I couldn't understand why A kept asking to meet up with me. Whenever she was in town, she'd invite me to go out with her and her friends. She told me to come to Baton Rouge and stay with her, but I never did. I didn't know what she wanted. But I wanted her, so badly. Like a teenager, the thought of the one night she spent in my bed distracted my body constantly.

The makeup artist moves away from the lead actress, back to her foldout chair with the rest of the makeup team, all slumped in their chairs and intently scrolling on their phones. Makeup artists are almost always women who don't seem to give a fuck about the movie or the director or the producers or whoever else is supposed to be important. I've always liked this about them. I go to stand behind them.

I look at P again and he's still watching me. I smile back at him. I miss him. I remember, also, how much I miss this: him, seeing me. I wish I could gauge better how he feels for me. Instead, I spin, I flail, waiting for this moment, his eyes on me affirming my existence, and yet still wishing for something more, for words.

A and I continued through August with flirtatious texts, with trying to meet up and sometimes meeting up, until one night in September, a few months ago, when I went out with her to a dance party and one of her friends hit on me. I wasn't interested in A's friend—though I momentarily tried to be—I was interested in A, in her beautiful clumsiness, in the way I felt when I danced close to her, in the way she smelled and how her eyes narrowed almost to a close when she smiled her infectious smile. But A and I didn't go home together that night, and the next day A texted me telling me how much her friend liked me and asking if it was okay if she gave them my number. I had to stop chasing A. I couldn't make her want me.

Recently, I told P he couldn't sleep with A again, even though I know he wants to, even though I think they're still texting. I try not to think of my insecurity. I try not to think about how all I want to do is have sex with A—or Jess, or someone who isn't P, so I can stop feeling like someone betrayed, like a woman—or write a film about my inaction, and I can do neither. In looking for a new way to relate to what had happened, different from what I'd seen in the movies, different from what I'd seen my parents do, I still somehow ended up here, alone. If I keep trying to be separate from my parents, from my family, will I still inherit only the same narratives, over and over again, cradled by the comfort of a familiar circle?

If only I could find my way back to myself.

James walks through the smoky bar back to his spot behind the monitor, which I can see from my position behind the seated makeup team. He pulls his headphones up from his neck, over his ears. A series of state-ments follows, from the mouths of different men in the room, *picture's up, alright, lock it up, roll camera, camera rolling, roll sound, sound speeds, mark it*, and then finally James: *action*. The room, packed full of people, is utterly silent as the actors move through their action, their dialogue, in front of us like a stage play. The lead actress is in her late forties, and the lead actor is in his early thirties—the characters are lovers, and this age difference is supposed to be something of significance in the film. In the scene, she's drunk, belligerent, and yelling at the lead actor.

I watch them sitting at the bar, her falling off her stool; I watch her yell-ing at him in front of me.

Then I look over at the monitor to see what James sees, the small rect-angle their actions will forever live in—I watch her yelling at him on the screen, and it's like they're not even in the same room as me anymore; I'm already watching the film.

imagineering

I sit on a slightly damp plastic bench inside a fake log, which moves forward in a contained stream of water. I'm in front and there are three rows behind me, kids with their parents and two rowdy teenagers in the back. We move through a cave-like tunnel of red rock, a conveyor belt carrying us up slowly, over a waterfall and outside. Now, we are atop a large hill, a landscape of reddish dirt and tufts of grass, mysteriously emanating a cheery tune. The skies are blue and clear and it's hot, but not as hot as New Orleans. On the banks are tiny treehouses and minia-ture gardens and clotheslines, too small for humans to tend. Briefly, we can see the park from an unusually panoramic vantage point—though, besides the castle, we can't see much beyond Frontier World. We slip down slight drops in the stream, hinting at our demise, and the kids behind me yelp, thinking it's the real thing.

Our log moves into an opening on the side of the hill, and my eyes adjust to the low light, though there are bright blue skies and hills of impossibly green grass signaling we are still outside, just a different kind of outside where everything looks like a cartoon. Trees create a canopy above us and, on the banks of the stream, birds and frogs serenade us with a very repetitive song. Downstream, a large bear with a blue shirt and red cap chuckles. Atop him stands a fox, wearing a vest, hat, trousers, and a menacing smile of sharp teeth. Both are diligently watching a rabbit, who stands unaware outside a small cabin like a traveler, a bindle resting on his shoulder. I know each turn, each small drop in the stream, so well, like the blocks of familiar Manhattan neighborhoods I traversed in combat boots throughout high school, walking to meet up with friends, to drink in parks, to kill time.

*

From first grade into college, I loved to draw. I filled journals with sketches of people I'd never seen next to moody attempts at poetry. I eroded sticks of charcoal and wore the black residue in the creases of my fingers with pride. One of the first things I ever learned to draw was Mickey Mouse's head. His formulaic proportions and the simple, heart-shaped contours of his face allowed my young hand to easily copy the image from a book. After much repetition from the original image, I came to memorize the shapes and their relation to each other and was ultimately able to render Mickey from memory. I drew him on the margins of school notebooks, paper tablecloths at restaurants with my family, birthday cards to my friends. It wasn't that I particularly cared for his cartoon persona or my relation to him—I was just pleased with how well I could draw him.

*

When we went to Disney World as a family, we were always paired with a tour guide in a plaid vest. As a kid, this experience of the park was one of the primary perks of my middle name. Usually our guide was Jim, a sweet, stout man who would take us through the back entrances of the rides and entertain us by pointing out "hidden Mickeys." He would tell us interesting facts about the rides and their design, though he would never get too technical, often resorting to the explanation that something was made possible by "Disney Magic." When I was a kid, I was sure this tendency of Jim's was not unlike the other deceptive games adults play to keep a child's innocent and expansive imagination alive. Like the Tooth Fairy or Santa, Jim seemed to want me to fully believe in Peter Pan and his ability to fly, even though I could clearly see the wires glinting in the lights of the parade.

*

According to the Oxford Living Dictionary, an "imagineer" is a "person who devises and implements a new or highly imaginative concept or technology, in particular one who devises the attractions in Walt Disney theme parks." When I was very little, I loved the idea of imagineering. When asked, I would tell people I wanted to be either an animator or an imagineer when I grew up. I had no idea there was a heavy science component to the latter (despite *engineer* being half the word)—I just loved the concept of becoming a professional in inhabiting the imagination. I preferred imaginary spaces to reality, finding freedom, or escape, in the vivid daydreams that would run through my mind like movies with no end. In these daydreams, my two best friends, both boys, and I would be a troop of superheroes roaming a magical version of New York City, sometimes in the likeness of the Power Rangers and sometimes looking like our scruffy selves, chasing each other around a sandy playground.

*

In the cartoonish interior of the ride, from inside the fiberglass log, we see the fox and bear—mannequins who move through their stilted motions on repeat—thwarted in their schemes to catch the rabbit, our vantage point continuously moving forward through the scenes on the artificial stream. The bear is tied up by his feet and arms to the branch of a tree while the rabbit bounds away, taunting him. Later, the fox stands beneath the bear, trying to hoist his large body up into a hole in a tree. The bear is saying, through a quiet speaker, in his dopey voice, he doesn't see anything in the hole, only bees. The rabbit laughs hysterically in a branch above. Our log jerks and stops, bumping up against another log in front of it, and momentarily we are paused watching the animals replay their actions again and again. Written sloppily on the tree like graffiti are the words "to the laughin' place" with an arrow pointed in the direction our log is inevitably heading. Soon, once the log in front of us has advanced far enough, the stream moves us quickly down into the darkness of the laughin' place, a cave-like space hanging with glow-in-the-dark beehives, bees buzzing around them in circles. I feel goose bumps rising on my arms from the chill air. In the cave the bear sways stupidly from side to side, balanced precariously on his butt with a beehive stuck on his nose. He screams repeatedly from the stings. Meanwhile, the rabbit lies on his back, holding his belly from laughter, completely unaware of the fox, who stands over him with a beehive, about to pounce. Maniacal laughter follows us as our log drops into a darker cave, with stalactites and stalagmites and water gushing from geysers, the cold spray dampening my shirt. Now, the fox stands proudly on the bank of the stream, holding a rope in one fist and the rabbit by his ears in the other. The rabbit's body is contained by a beehive, oozing yellow honey.

*

By my teens the charm of "Disney Magic" had worn off and I was beginning to suspect that, instead of protecting me and my siblings' innocence, Jim was sometimes hiding the secrets of the company or at least the reality of how things were done. One time, when I was in high school, we were about to get on the Winnie the Pooh ride (ironically, I guess, since we were old for that) when, from what we could understand, someone in front of us in line fell onto the track as the cars were moving. The ride came to a jarring stop. I couldn't see the person, so I couldn't tell how old they were or if they'd actually been run over or trapped by one of the cars. I could only see people crowded around the track, speaking down into it in hushed, concerned tones. The looped sing-songy music continued over the speakers as Jim quickly ushered us away from the ride and insisted nothing had happened, no one had fallen into the track, and the ride was simply experiencing technical difficulties. We wondered aloud throughout the following days if the person was okay, but Jim never told us what, exactly, had happened. Staring down at the dark pit into which the person had fallen, seeing the distraught faces of their loved ones, I worried the injuries they'd sustained would ruin more than their vacation. I realized that, for Jim, Disney Magic could at times function as a lie in the form of make-believe.

*

From ages eight to eleven, when I was a tomboy with Alex, our peers—and adults—thought we were strange, but this didn't matter because we had each other and knew we were actually very cool. In fact, the less we cared about what other people thought of us, the cooler we felt, a private feeling we shared. I carried this with me, even after Alex moved away and we lost touch, even after I grew more ashamed of the moment in my life when I looked, or tried to look, like a boy. Going into high school, I was shy and weird and didn't fit easily into any friend group, a floater, but I cultivated a certain pride in not being "normal," and with this came a rejection of Disney. I would not be an animator; I would not be an imagineer. When I was in tenth grade, my interest in drawing channeled into an obsession with street art, which I thought of as wholly in opposition to Disney, against everything mainstream, as it was an art form entirely for public consumption, supposedly not for sale. I traced and cut stencil graffiti with an X-ACTO in art class and tagged SKANK in dripping markers all over the blue city mailboxes near my school and worshiped Basquiat, getting his tag, "SAMO," tattooed on my inner lip. The irony escaped me at the time—a white girl sitting in the comfort of my bedroom on the Upper West Side, dreaming of becoming Basquiat, whose New York City (coming of age as a Black man in the 1970s Lower East Side, amidst early hip-hop and punk, houselessness, heroin) differed so greatly from mine. I also didn't know then how the art world chewed him up, isolated him, because art, no matter how subversive, is for sale. (And I didn't know how even later, in my twenties, I would see Basquiat's work adorning T-shirts at UNIQLO just rows away from the store's similarly styled Disney collection.)

*

In 1958 the nature documentary *White Wilderness*, produced by Walt Disney Productions, won the Academy Award for Best Documentary

Feature. The film contains the first photographic evidence of mass lemming suicide, a widely held legend that, despite the documentation,
turns out to be false. "It's a shame that that sort of thing has to happen,"
my grandfather, Roy E., said to CBC many years later when asked how
they got the footage. My younger brother told me about the excerpt,
which he'd heard in an episode of a podcast, *Science Vs*, that debunks
the cultural myth of lemming suicide, which *White Wilderness* largely
contributed to. How strange it is to hear my grandfather's voice as he
calmly intones, "As I recall, they did stage some of that . . . We lost a few
lemmings, okay, the lemmings probably would've gotten lost anyway."
In the film hordes of lemmings tumble down a cliffside as the narrator
explains their "suicidal" journey, "creating tiny avalanches of sliding
soil and rocks" as they slip reluctantly to their deaths, some clinging
desperately to the face of the cliff and trying to climb back up. Some
lemmings soar from considerable heights through the air, plopping
down into the water below. In the '80s one of the cameramen admitted
that the filmmakers of *Wild Wilderness* threw the small creatures off the
cliff to recreate what they believed to be reality. In one overhead shot of
the action, a medium shot looking down at the lemmings on the brink
of the cliff, you can sense the off-screen presence of the filmmakers,
just beyond the frame, throwing and pushing the lemmings over the
edge—"movie magic" or, perhaps, *Disney Magic*.

*

I loved going to Disney World. It was hard for me to pretend I no longer
loved it. I was a teenager who wanted to be a punk, or something edgier
than I was: a privileged private school kid and rule-abider who loved
Disney World. I loved riding the rides but, even more so, I loved simply
walking around the different parks, especially the Magic Kingdom and
Epcot. I loved that each place was like being inside a different film; you
could freely roam the set, becoming the characters. I loved the amount
of detail carefully considered in the crafting of each world: a volcano
with a glowing rim of lava in Epcot's Mexico, smoke teeming out against
a fake night sky; a quill pen and leather-bound books atop a wooden

desk inside the Swiss Family Robinson's treehouse, a structure cobbled together from ship parts, bamboo, and dried palmetto leaves; the hairy leg of a pirate hanging just above you as your boat drifts under the bridge he sits on, through the dark night of the Pirates of the Caribbean ride. Long before it was made into a movie, the Pirates of the Caribbean ride was one of my first introductions to what happens to bodies after life leaves them. I remember how the image of skeletons splayed out on the beach, a sword through one's rib cage, fueled my young nightmares. Floating into the cool depths of the ride's nighttime interior, your plastic vessel moves between a large pirate ship and a towering fort, bombs flying overhead and plunking into the water on either side of you. The boat moves down a canal through the town, and you watch fearfully as chaos erupts, the pirates ravaging their way through the space, looting houses and tormenting the townspeople. One pirate auctions off hens to a group of male bidders—not too long ago, when I was little, the "hens" spoken of were animatronic women, not chickens—and later the whole town is consumed in flames as the robots sing "Yo Ho (A Pirate's Life for Me)." On a plastic boat, an aquatic conveyor belt moving you haltingly forward through space and time, the action of the pirates envelops you; the ride allows you to live inside a movie.

*

In college, after just one semester of Intro to Drawing, I concluded I was not a true visual artist. For the class's final project, we had to draw a proportionally accurate, life-sized nude self-portrait. I worked very hard on mine, studying closely the curves and shadows of my face, my arms, my breasts, measuring the distance of my proportions with a ruler. However, when we presented our projects, pinning them up on the gray walls of the drafty, dimly lit art room, I realized for many others in my class, drawing was not such an onerous, precise task as it was for me. There was something looser about the lines of these other drawings, something expressive, alive, about their work I thought my drawing did not possess. When I drew I was often working from another image, trying my best to imitate it. I copied the gestures of another artist—memorizing how to draw Mickey or stenciling over one of Basquiat's crowns—instead of creating something original. After that class I stopped drawing completely.

Looking back at my final artwork, after pulling the rolled-up self-portrait from the closet in my mom's apartment where it now lives, I've grown a new fondness for the piece. In the drawing I stand stark naked except for socks, in contrapposto, facing the viewer, staring directly forward like a challenge, as I let my bra fall to the floor from an open hand. The person in the drawing is me but so much braver than I am—the real me would drop my eyes and bring my arms to cover my chest. When I dismissed the sketch so quickly for its craft, I'd forgotten what I liked about drawing in the first place: how it allowed me to create an imaginary world, how it allowed me to reinvent my identity. Writing has always had a similar attraction for me, allowing me the freedom to become simply a voice, unattached from expectations of the way I dress, the way I talk, the way I am inside my gendered body. With drawing, with writing, I could uncover myself, the person I longed to be.

*

In Judith Butler's essay "Imitation and Gender Insubordination," she writes: *Gender is a kind of imitation for which there is no original.* At first, our performance as kids was a facet of our imaginary life—Alex and I were boys, instead of princesses. But the imaginary world was much larger than us. Tapping into a collective imagination, we questioned a world that imagined us as girls in the first place.

*

Our log begins another slow climb up a conveyor belt, beneath two menacing crows, one of which addresses us, *Everybody's got a laughin' place* . . . We move slowly upward through a tunnel toward the real outdoors, a circle of sky we can see far above. The teens in back are howling dramatically in jokey anticipation. Near the top the rabbit pleads for the fox not to throw him in the briar patch. The fox threatens to hang him, and the rabbit screams, *That's alright, Br'er Fox—hang me if you gotta! But please,* please, *don't fling me in that briar patch!* At those words our log drops, almost weightless, toward the thorny briar patch below, and everyone screams. I scream, even though I knew it was coming, flinging my arms up to feel the drop. A light flashes to take our picture.

*

In her essay "On Imagination," the poet Mary Ruefle says that, for her, there is no difference between thinking and imagining. Though common sense and rational thinking are often thought of as oppositional to imaginary and magical thinking, Ruefle suggests, there is really no distinction. The imagination, she says, is what tells us we are safe or that our belongings are really our belongings. Ruefle reminds us that the imagination can both create and destroy; it can work toward both good and bad ends.

*

Of course, there's the question of who gets to imagine. Or rather whose imagination is emphasized. It's not surprising that, for a large portion of Disney's history, this pool was limited—the imagination one encounters in the parks and in many of the original Disney films is, like its founder, overwhelmingly white and male. In a letter written in 1938, published recently by *Vox*, to a young woman applying for a creative position at Disney, the company replied, "Women do not do any of the creative work in connection with preparing the cartoons for the screen, as that work is performed entirely by young men. For this reason girls are not considered for the training school." In the early days of Disney hand-drawn animation, women were only permitted to work in the all-female (and all-white) Ink and Paint Department.[1] There, they worked tirelessly, often through the night, painting with detail each of the individual cells that made up films such as *Snow White*.[2] "The girls," as Walt called them, were required to undergo months of rigorous unpaid training before their official, and in no way guaranteed, acceptance into the program. Similar to the work performed by the first editors of film—"film joiners" and "negative cutters," who were primarily working-class women whose names did not appear in the credits of the films they worked on—inking and painting was time-consuming and intricate and, therefore, considered suitable women's work, much like sewing.

*

By my senior year of college, I'd decided to major in film studies, and I was one of the nineteen students in my grade who chose to direct a thesis film. There were three other women in the group. The thesis shoots were thought of as a good environment to learn, and often students filled roles they had little experience in but were hoping to pursue professionally. I'd put my name into the mix since cinematography appealed to me and I'd had some experience with a camera. The summer before senior year, I emailed my whole class, expressing enthusiasm for the position. Only one person emailed me back asking me to shoot his thesis, but a few weeks before the shoot, he replaced me with his male friend Ben, who was a photography major. I wasn't confident enough about my abilities as a cinematographer to protest. I quietly accepted my demotion to first assistant camera, wishing I'd never sent that desperate email in the first place.

On set Ben, accustomed to shooting still images, would often press "record" and look completely away from the monitor. This tendency resulted in many shots with the boom dropping into the top of the frame, a few shots with a crew member standing in the frame for the whole take, and a lot of schadenfreude on my part. I never, however, got serious about my desire to be a cinematographer again.

Both in college and, later, on professional sets, I became familiar with the hierarchical, almost militaristic, nature of the male-dominated filmmaking industry. When I was learning, I soon understood I should never ask questions. I tried not to reveal my weaknesses, which would make me vulnerable to men who already thought I wasn't competent and who were so quick to explain things even when I didn't ask. On a set for a short film, I was a camera assistant and I noticed how the guys in my department always stepped around me, never really looking at me or addressing me directly. "Boys," they called each other, telling corny jokes about the uselessness of the other departments among other things, once even referring to something gross as *smelling like vagina*.

I don't know, however, what it's like to be a person of color on these often very white film sets. I don't know what it's like to be a person of color in this white industry.

*

Disney's first Black animator, Floyd Norman, was hired in the mid-1950s. Until 2020 Disney had never produced an animated film directed by a person of color (the first being *Soul*, a Pixar film codirected by Kemp Powers).

*

Disney's live action–animated hybrid film *Song of the South* was released in 1946. The film is based on the Uncle Remus stories, recorded and adapted by author Joel Chandler Harris, and follows a young white boy, Johnny, as he moves with his mother to his grandmother's plantation in Georgia. On the plantation Johnny is entertained and taught life lessons by Uncle Remus, who narrates the animated, musical stories of Br'er Rabbit and his many adventures. The film never specifies the time period in which it is set and, therefore, it's disturbingly unclear what Uncle Remus's status on the plantation is—whether he's enslaved or an employee of Johnny's grandmother—while his relationship with the white people in the film is depicted as overwhelmingly positive. Following the film's release, Walter Francis White, the executive secretary of the NAACP, released a statement saying that the NAACP lauded the technical achievements of the film but "regrets, however, that in an effort neither to offend audiences in the North or South, the production helps to perpetuate a dangerously glorified picture of slavery . . . [the film] unfortunately gives the impression of an idyllic master-slave relationship which is a distortion of the facts." The film was picketed in New York City, and Adam Clayton Powell Jr. wrote to the commissioner of licenses that the film was "an insult to American minorities." Due to segregation laws, James Baskett, Uncle Remus in the film, and the other African American cast members were not present at the premiere in Atlanta, which was reportedly attended by over five thousand people. Disney rereleased *Song of the South* in theaters a few more times, in 1956, 1972, 1980, and 1986, and each time it was a financial success. Since the rerelease in 1986, however, the film has been locked in the "Disney vault" and has never been released in the United States on any home video format.[3]

The Splash Mountain ride opened at Disneyland on July 17th, 1989, and at Disney World on July 17th, 1992. Despite Disney's actions to keep the film inaccessible to the American public since the '80s, over 75 million dollars was reportedly spent to build the original Splash Mountain attraction in Disneyland, based on *Song of the South*. It was one of my favorite rides when I was a child, but I had no clue what the narrative of the ride had been inspired by—I'd never seen nor heard of a film called *Song of the South* and yet, because of Splash Mountain, I came to know the songs from the film by heart. In "Zip-A-Dee-Doo-Dah," the tune that won *Song of the South* the 1948 Oscar for best original song, James Baskett sings about how great life is, proclaiming that it's the truth, it's actual. Though the song plays throughout Splash Mountain, Uncle Remus's likeness is notably absent—only mechanical versions of Br'er Rabbit and the other critters from Uncle Remus's stories inhabit the constructed landscape of the ride.

Also missing from the ride is a significant element of one of the subplots of *Song of the South*: the technique Br'er Fox uses to finally catch Br'er Rabbit, the "tar baby" the original fable is named for. In both Uncle Remus's fable "Br'er Rabbit and the Tar Baby" and *Song of the South*, the fox shapes and dresses up a lump of tar to look like a child, placing the figure on the side of the road. The rabbit, thinking the lump of tar is a child with bad manners when it doesn't respond to him, hits it and gets stuck to it. The rabbit is ultimately able to escape by convincing the fox, through reverse psychology, to throw him in the briar patch, a treacherous place the rabbit is able to navigate easily because it's where he grew up.

Asked how she chose the title for her 1981 novel, Toni Morrison explained that "tar baby" was a derogatory term she remembered white people using for Black children, particularly Black girls. However, she had since come to redefine the term to mean an important or holy site, as a "black woman who can hold things together."[4] Politicians such as former Mississippi governor Haley Barbour, Mitt Romney, and quite a few others have taken criticism for using the term in the past decades to mean a "sticky situation."

On the Splash Mountain ride, the imagineers replaced the offensive "tar baby" from the film with another sticky object the fox uses to entrap the rabbit: a beehive, oozing honey.

In her foreword to *Tar Baby*, Morrison refers to the Uncle Remus fable, which she finds very puzzling. She wonders how the farmer (the fox) knows the rabbit will react the way he does to the decoy and why the tar is dressed as a little girl, even comparing the relationship between the rabbit and the tar baby to a love story. After the rabbit is thrown in the briar patch, Morrison writes, *The figure of tar, having done its work, falls out of the action of the tale, yet remains not only as its strange, silent center, but also as the sticky mediator between master and peasant, plantation owner and slave. Constructed by the farmer to foil and entrap, it moves beyond trickery to art.*

What is the truth Disney's Uncle Remus sings of? What was the version of the South, of America, Walt imagined?

What happens to a story whose origins have been so willfully obscured?

*

Last year I took a "fossil free" bus tour of the area of Louisiana along the Mississippi River between New Orleans and Baton Rouge known as "Cancer Alley." I stared out the tinted window at plantation houses, surrounded by haunting oak trees, and petrochemical plants with their huge towers spouting flames and fumes. Leon Waters, a New Orleans historian who was leading the tour, stood at the front of the bus, explaining the history of Cancer Alley. The area is named for the disease more and more residents have found themselves afflicted with due to the emissions they've been exposed to by the many refineries and petrochemical plants along the River. One-third of Louisiana's Black residents live in the Mississippi corridor region, many of them descendants of enslaved people forced to work the land along the Mississippi River—on plantation land that has since been purchased by Shell and ExxonMobil.[5]

I watched Waters, at the front of the bus, pushing his glasses up the bridge of his nose, firmly holding onto the back of a seat as our bus coiled around the turns in the road, mirroring the movements of the Mississippi River. He told us about the plantations along River Road, which drive tourism to the heavily polluted region, each plantation boasting its own tour of its historic premises. On these plantations famous films have been shot and many elaborate weddings are still thrown. Some are B&Bs. The websites for these plantations mention the fact of slavery in passing, if at all. The site for the Oak Alley plantation reads: "Feel the gentle breeze of Southern hospitality on a tour that takes you back to the glory of the Old South! . . . Travel past Whitney, Evergreen, Felicity & St. Joseph Plantations, ghosts of the past that front the Mississippi River, where rich crops of sugar cane, cotton and indigo from these fertile lands once traveled to ports of trade."

A version of the South, imagined, quite similar to the one presented in *Song of the South*. Waters told us of how, on these plantation tours, you will be asked to admire the Greek revival architecture, the decadent dining rooms, the intricate woodwork, the design of the china. Going to one of these plantations and admiring the china, Waters posited, is like going to Auschwitz and admiring the polish of a Nazi's boot.[6] How could this statement seem both surprising and yet so obvious? So true?

*

At Disney World you encounter a cross section of America—families who've traveled from all over this big country, families who've maxed out credit cards paying the absurdly steep $126 daily per-person entrance fee, families who've come to experience the "magic." In 2017, 20.45 million visitors went to Disney World's Magic Kingdom theme park.[7] *Explore Lands of Endless Enchantment, Where Your Fantasy Becomes a Reality,* exclaims the Magic Kingdom's website.

"I don't want the public to see the world they live in while they're in the park. I want them to feel they're in another world," Walt said.

*

There's a framed photo hanging in the hallway of my mom's apartment in Manhattan, among many others, of my mom and her three siblings standing, as always, in ascending order of age and height, on a mound of dirt. That very mound of dirt would become Cinderella's castle at Disney World in Orlando. On top of all that soil, wet earth that was once marsh, the Magic Kingdom would exist. What is more beautiful, the dark mystery of the swamp, or the marketable fantasy built on top of it?

*

I find, through the internet, fragments of truth about my ancestors. Most of what I know regarding my dead relatives comes through these impersonal channels. Sitting at the desk in my living room, the air conditioning churning away in an attempt to fight the reality of the oncoming New Orleans summer, I come across a 2011 article in the *New York Times* called "And Now a Word From the Director," by Manohla Dargis, that begins: "In 1938, a month after the Nazi assault on German Jews known as Kristallnacht made headlines across the world, Walt Disney gave Hitler's pet filmmaker, Leni Riefenstahl, a tour of his studio . . . In his biography 'Leni' Steven Bach writes that when she returned to Germany, she praised Disney for receiving her, saying, it 'was gratifying to learn how thoroughly proper Americans distance themselves from the smear campaigns of the Jews.'"

I've never heard this fact before and, reading this article for the first time, I'm deeply confused by my lack of familiarity with the truth of my name. My mom has told me she is certain Walt was an anti-Semite—she's even said so more publicly and received flak from some of our relatives for this—and for much of my life I've heard the cultural wisecracks about Walt's bigotry just as I've heard of his supposed cryogenic freezing: as if it's a myth. I've never before been faced with any of the actual details of this narrative. I stare at the computer screen, my legs pulled to my chest, feeling sick, feeling unsure of how to be myself.

*

When I was a kid, I went to the park so many times that reality often reminded me of Disney World instead of the other way around. This still happens. I'll be walking down a quaint main street somewhere in America on a road trip with P and I'll think *this reminds me so much of the Magic Kingdom.* I'll be lurching through a subway tunnel, staring out the window, and realize I'm searching the darkness for some sign of animatronic life. This impulse disturbs me. In *Simulacra and Simulations* (1981), Jean Baudrillard writes, "Disneyland is presented as imaginary in order to make us believe that the rest is real, when in fact all of Los Angeles and the America surrounding it are no longer real, but of the order of the hyper-real and of simulation."

*

Occasionally, friends or professors in college, upon hearing I was majoring in film, would say something like, "Ah, the family business . . ." and I would find myself startled, forgetting what my middle name is so well known for. Or perhaps not forgetting, but wanting to separate my pursuit of the medium from what my family has done. It was hard for me to admit that, once upon a time, I'd been undeniably enchanted by all my ancestors created—I had fallen for the Disney Magic, and it made me want to be an imagineer. It was not until I was older that I realized how certain imaginations are emphasized in this country, how only these imaginations are accepted as reality.

*

Mary Reufle says our imagination tells us our belongings are our belongings. It is our collective imagination then, as Americans, that allows us to believe we own the land at all. In "Colors of the Wind," Disney's Pocahontas addresses the colonizer and his belief that he owns whatever land he sets foot on, as if the earth is not alive, as if it's something dead to be claimed—and this rings true, though her animated narrative is so different from that of the real-life teenager she was modeled after. A Houma chief I met recently, speaking of the legal hoops her tribe is required to go through to receive federal recognition, told me that all these documents they have to file, all these laws they have to abide by, are *fake*. Everything that has happened since white people arrived here on this land, she told me, is fake. The Indian Removal Act of 1830 pushed the Houma people—originally located near present-day Baton Rouge—to the edges of Louisiana, the coastal bayous, where they learned to live off the land, now sinking into the Gulf. Along with sea-level rise, subsidence, caused by the leveeing of the Mississippi River and incessant digging of manmade canals through the marsh by oil companies, is forcing these communities to relocate once again. When the BP oil spill decimated their fisheries, wetlands, and livelihoods in 2010, the United Houma Nation was unable to collect damages from BP, because they are not officially recognized by the U.S. government.[8] For over thirty years, they have been fighting for recognition, the government citing a lack of proof that the Houma people of today are related to the Houma tribe encountered by French colonialist Robert de La Salle.[9] The proof of their existence, therefore, lies within this white man's word and what he determined, many years ago, to be Houma. For the U.S. government, the proof has nothing to do with the 17,000 Houma people now proclaiming *we exist*.

*

Walt's 1955 opening day speech for Disneyland culminates: "Disneyland is dedicated to the ideals, the dreams and the hard facts that have created America . . . with the hope that it will be a source of joy and inspiration to all the world."

*

In his essay "The Creative Process," James Baldwin writes about how the artist's intention as well as burden in life is that they must cultivate a state of being alone. They are alone, Baldwin posits, because they see and understand the reality of the world in a way society refuses to accept. It's the job of the artist to attempt to reveal this deeper, unseen reality to others. Baldwin finishes his essay: *Societies never know it, but the war of an artist with his society is a lover's war, and he does, at his best, what lovers do, which is to reveal the beloved to himself and, with that revelation, to make freedom real.*

*

The imagination, something that for the most part has allowed me to be free, has also been used to limit or prevent the freedom of others. I've found myself desperately hoping to dissociate myself from the negative powers of the imagination, from my ancestors who oppressed people through art. I know this is not honest. Really, I'm still not sure how to weave together these parts of my identity, though I'll keep trying. I'll continue trying to find a way for these contradictory truths to live within me—to remember where I learned to imagine, where I came from, as I hope, at the same time, to reimagine the world as it's been presented to me.

*

After the log takes its big dive, we splash into a slower stream outside, floating past onlookers on the bridge above: children considering if the drop is as scary as it seems, adults wondering how it could possibly be worth the hour-long wait. Now that the drop is over with, the ride feels so calm and everyone talks about how they want to do it again, even if most of the experience was filled with dread. Our log passes a waterfall, which splashes some, and a small drop descends into the interior of the ride one last time. Inside, it's dark and the big fake sky glows orange like a sunset. A large steamboat tips back and forth and, on it, a variety of creatures enthusiastically dance and sing. Geese hold their skirts in their wings and kick up their feet, a frog strums a cello, and chickens wave tambourines in the air. As a chorus, they sing, *Zip-a-dee-doo-dah, zip-a-dee-ay!* We float past the fox and the bear, stuck painfully in the briar patch, and the rabbit, resting with his hands behind his head, in front of his cabin, singing along with the chorus. As our log moves out to the waiting area, where we'll get off the ride, we move past a wooden panel painted with a message—it's lit up by the sun filtering in from the outside waiting area. In the glare it reads, *It's the truth, it's actual* . . .

delta dawn

a tornado last night
i think we were one of those he says
driving past downed trees on st. claude
get a room howled the bros on frenchmen street
between our wet faces he said he wanted kids with me
the wind, the rain, his hands the same size as mine
i told him i loved him so quietly, the words more breath than sound
but knew he heard me

His mouth. That is where I am when I realize we're moving, the ground
beneath us slowly shifting in space. The bar and the stools we sit on are
rotating, and the angle from which I see the room changes each time I
resurface from M's mouth, M's eyes, that look that makes me want to
forget my life. In the six years I've lived in New Orleans, I've never been
to Carousel Bar before, a famous spot in the Quarter, and now I'm a
tourist in my own city. Everyone thinks I'm French because he is and I
don't correct them because it's fun to be a person I don't know.
Rotating is our motion, we circle each other:
Around fluorescent-lit gas station aisles, looking for Zapps chips
and tall cans of Bud Light for the long ride home after a shoot, when

we can finally let our hands touch in the darkness of the car while
another crew member drives.

On the rickety structure, a miniature lighthouse on the levee at the
End of the World. We climb to the top, the metal landing with a
flashing blue light at its center. I move away from him and he moves
toward me, we teeter above the River, we step in circles on the grated
metal surface, blue intermittently streaking across our faces.

In the rain, on a street corner, the night the wind tears apart the trees
and the power lines and I say I love him even though I've known him
just a week, even though each night I return to P in our apartment.

On the dance floor at Vaughn's, I play Whitney Houston on the jukebox,
we move around each other again and again on the last night of the
shoot, when we've stopped pretending in front of the rest of the crew.
We kiss, hold each other, in circles. I don't know which one of us is
moving, I don't know what is creating the centripetal force between
us, but I am dizzy, I forget there is movement other than spinning, I
forget there is forward motion.

M's job is to translate life into images. That's what he came to do for us
when we flew him from Paris to New Orleans in October 2019. I watched
his cinematography reel only a week before he arrived. Our original DP
had gotten another job that paid too much for her to turn down, and a
filmmaker friend had recommended M to us. We knew very little about
him but, for some reason, we trusted her fully—a Swiss girl we'd known
for only a few days, at a film festival, who seemed like the kind of person
we'd be friends with. I'd been producing the documentary for over a year,
and this was our last big, month-long shoot. I'd spent weeks planning
and scheduling for it. We were praying M would work out.

On the Thursday before the shoot, I drove the rental to pick M up from
the airport, and it was raining so hard. It was still day but the sky was
black. His plane circled and circled above the dark clouds, running out
of fuel, and was redirected to Jackson, Mississippi. I knew this only
from the internet, from checking his flight information again and
again as I sat in the car at a gas station near the airport.

I drove back and waited with Lara, the director, at her house. We
picked at pasta she'd made for M, drank wine, and wondered if he'd
get here in time for the first day of the shoot.

Sitting in Lara's kitchen, I got a call from an unknown number. It was
M, the first time I heard his voice, his accent, and he was laughing
a lot. Maybe he was nervous. I was. He told me they were still on
the plane, waiting to take off again for New Orleans. I apologized
profusely for his terrible flight, as if it were my fault, but he just
laughed so I laughed too. In his voice there was understanding, even
though we were both stumbling over our words, accidentally cutting
each other off.

An hour later Lara and I happened to walk out to the street just as
his taxi pulled up. He was still laughing and was younger than I'd
imagined; he looked around my age, twenty-eight. He had black-
brown curls streaked with a few strands of gray. They fell into his
face, and he tucked them behind his ear. Dark stubble framed his
lips. We went inside and sat on Lara's living room floor with plates of
pasta. I quickly noticed he struggled a little with English and worried
this might be a problem on set, for him to follow the interviews. But I
liked the way there was no pretentiousness about him. I also liked the
way he laughed, the sound tumbling out of him like water bubbling
out of a faucet.

the morning after the tornado
we get coffee before the shoot and a little girl who looks like me
is looking at us
he says *you still want one of those with me*
i don't at all it's crazy
but i still like when he says this   a form of adoration i'm not used to
his smell seeps into me so easily   i've never craved the smell of
perfume & cigarettes
my old red truck is parked on my street—i sold it years ago for
cash—i cry   hold its metal in my
arms like a lost friend

i start smoking again
smoking is breathing him in
word by word
he translates a french song for me standing naked by the window
camel blue hanging from
his mouth   i tell him people would pay good money for this
you know i don't even like french i say to p *i don't even like paris*
this is true
at night in my dream state i hold someone and i don't know who
p's hands are so much bigger than mine
the room slowly turning he says to the girl next to us at the bar *doesn't*
this look like love?

I'm in the shower, steam filling the bathroom because somehow it's
winter in New Orleans again and the apartment I share with P gets so
cold, when these words come back to me like I never lost them: *Me . . .*
I'm scared of everything. I'm scared of what I saw, I'm scared of what
I did, about who I am and most of all I'm scared of walking out of this
room and never feeling, the rest of my whole life, the way I feel when I'm
with you. At first I'm not sure where these sentences come from. I feel
like I've created them though I know I haven't—the familiar intona-
tions echo deep inside of me like yearning. Then I see her: Baby, her
curly brown hair and the white linen of her shirt as she sits in a chair
and looks up at Johnny, her nostrils flaring as these words pour out of
her, her voice cracking on the last line. How I ached to watch Johnny/
Patrick Swayze move his hand down the side of Baby/Jennifer Grey's
torso, annoyed when he is met with her uncontrollable laughter, as they
practice the dance together, as she learns to move fluidly with him,
until he touches her side and she doesn't laugh anymore. I've turned
around in my mind so many times the reasons I found these kinds of
films appealing when I was younger. For years I was embarrassed by
this obsession. *Dirty Dancing, You've Got Mail, Runaway Bride, Sleepless*
in Seattle, Notting Hill, Pretty Woman, Love Actually—all these movies
contain lines like these that live in the corners of my brain. *Nobody puts*

baby in . . . oh, it's so stupid. Now, I realize I loved these romantic films because they presented an unreal world with a certain order, where things are *meant to happen*, where people are *meant to be*, where every coincidence has weight in one's life. At Vaughn's, when the six of us crew members gather for our mini wrap party at the end of the October shoot, I put the *Dirty Dancing* song on the jukebox as a joke. *Now, I've had the time of my life* . . . Bill Medley croons from the speakers, and M rolls his eyes and tells me, on that note, he's going for a cigarette. He gets to the door, though, sees all of us dancing, and he pauses. He dances back to me, really going for it, pulling me to him, and I laugh and laugh because it's crazy. *You're wild!* Baby exclaims when Johnny busts the window of the car when he's forgotten the keys inside. I've never met anyone like M, so free, like a character in a movie I used to watch on repeat.

i watch the monitor while he moves with the camera at the community dance in baton rouge   seeing what he sees   feeling the movements of his body as the frame moves   like we are dancing together
on set i try not to look at him too much   try to speak to him like another crew member
when he works he is so serious   furrowed brow   pursed lips
baton rouge: his accent makes it into a place far away from here
again and again he reminds me he is swiss not french
oh-la-la you're scared of everything he says with a laugh
he sneaks us to the top floor of a fancy hotel on canal street so we can see the River
from the 47th floor   i've never seen it like that before   snaking with no end
interior / exterior   we move from bar to bar without logic / with intent
we run   an imagined camera rotating around us like we're in the *we found love in a hopeless place* music video   like we're jack and rose as ocean permeates the ship   like we're simba and nala somersaulting over each other into a green clearing
he says he would never allow an open

relationship if we were together
later he says this is true but also the line he thought might seduce me
he says I'm the best producer he's ever worked with—another line
that works
p buys me sunflowers brings me bagels in bed is sweeter than he's
ever been in our
five and a half years   even though i tell him everything
for the first time p asks me to marry him
but then plays it off as a joke

I usually find it funny that P is more objectified than I am, because
he's tall, beautiful, and flirtatious. I love the way older women and
men catcall him when he strolls through the Quarter in a short dress
and how attractive people shoot him looks across bars. *A tall drink
of water.* Sometimes, though, I find myself jealous of this attention.
Sometimes, I feel invisible beside him. Then I feel like I have to check
in with him to make sure it's okay I look like this, invisible to others.
For over a year now, since he slept with A, I've felt this more acutely.
Am I invisible to him? He assures me I am not. But I can't help but
notice how *cute* the girls he's drawn to are, how girlish.
In my mind I've looked like this forever. In reality I've looked like this,
really looked like this as an adult, for a few years. That is, I had long hair
for a while, used to wear dresses, lipstick sometimes. I didn't notice the
exact moment when it happened: the subtle shift in the way men's eyes
observed me. At some point after I started looking how I felt inside,
men stopped looking at me when I walked down the street—my body
ceased to be an invitation. When my mom talks about the experience
of aging as a woman, she usually refers to this: you suddenly fill space
differently, simply in how other eyes perceive you. Sometimes she
describes this ordeal quite gravely, like it's a form of death.
I enjoy this new existence for the most part, being a neutral body.
Though my body hasn't changed, really, the way it's understood has—
because I shave my head, because I wear boyish clothes. Like when
I was twelve, I now get called *sir, brother, man* by strangers, who

quickly correct themselves, far more embarrassed than I am by their utterances, whatever these words mean to them.

In M's presence, though, I am no longer neutral. I am sexy, but as I am—or perhaps because of who I am. His first crush, when he was eight in Geneva, *was a garçon manqué like you*, he says. A tomboy, like I was at that age. In French, it means literally a *missing* or *failed* boy. I never knew someone drawn to my failure or, rather, my attempt. In *The Pure and The Impure*, Colette writes, "I am alluding to a genuine mental hermaphroditism which burdens certain highly complex human beings." The narrator is talking about how she's hoping to rid herself of this cerebral ambiguity to become more of a woman. I like this idea, though, as if a state of being intellectually nonbinary comes with difficulty but also enlightenment.

We are making a film about three young women coming of age in Louisiana as they learn about how identity is bound to place and how their River has been managed and controlled. We film with the three teenagers in swamps and coastal bayous, in the teenagers' homes, at their schools. We drive in two cars filled to the brim with equipment, the three teens, and the six of us—the sound person, the camera assistant, Lara, the other producer, M, and me—for hours and hours each day. M couldn't possibly know where we are in relation to New Orleans, because it took me years to get it. It took me so long to understand all this land exists because of the River and that everything here relates to it. A week into the shoot, on Saturday night after a long day of filming with the teenagers on two small boats in the Mississippi River, M and I unload the camera equipment at Lara's house. Everyone else is occupied, dropping off the teenagers at their homes, and somehow M and I are alone, drinking beers and lugging cases of camera equipment. After, we get dinner at a nearby dive bar. I can barely eat. I'm so exhausted, and it takes only one whiskey for me to feel drunk. P has been gone for a few days, in Maine for work, and flies back to New Orleans tonight. Soon, it's 10:30 p.m. and he's landed. I don't respond to his calls or texts.

Instead, I tell M that, all day, I'd been wishing to be on the same boat as him. He was on the boat with the camera and other crew members, and I was crouching down in the boat they were filming, with the three teenagers—I had to lie at their feet so I wouldn't be in the frame. I stared at clear blue sky as we skated on brown water past barges whose size I'd never truly comprehended from land, towering over us, whose wakes pitched our boat, bumping my head against the sandpaper surface of the deck.

Over a year has gone by since the whole thing started with A; a few months earlier, during summer, I read their texts on P's computer. I found out he'd been continuing to flirt with her and secretly asking her to have a threesome with us, even though I'd already been rejected by her and the idea made me seasick. So finally I slept with someone else, with J on the riverbank, with a nonfeeling vengefulness that scared me. But this, with M, is different. With this, there is only feeling. M tells me all the important women in his life have been fish. I hate astrology—this is a crucial aspect of my identity, being one of the only people I know to hate astrology. Not knowing my chart makes me feel like I'm not really a woman. How many women do you know who don't know their charts? But then M asks me when my birthday is, and I say March 12th and suddenly I want to believe. I want to be a fish. I want M to be the water.

I don't know how this happened but it feels true. True because I put my phone on silent and bury it in my backpack like I've forgotten who I love / who I am. Maybe truth is this: losing oneself.

Later, we walk down a dark, empty street near the French Quarter, and I try to explain to M what a motto is because I used it in a sentence and he didn't understand. Words you live by. Drake, *yolo*. He says, *ah, like my name, like a maxim*. There was always a thin line for me between what was possible and what was not; I feel as if I just needed M to pull me over the border.

when we are alone we eat fast food: rally's mcdonald's gerald's
an all-night diner where i get biscuit bacon eggs with too much butter

i want to be american but only for him
he asks me to repeat words *panavision, bomber jacket, bacon*
cheeseburger i feel i take
the music out of words but he says i add my own
he shaves my head with his clippers accidentally leaving so many
hairs long goofily sticking
up off my skull
i say *i don't think i want to have kids with anyone*
he says i will because he knows my way is to be scared of everything
but brave   he knew this for sure when i showed up to his place with a
bag of clothes on his final sunday morning
i want to tell him firmly no
but it's our last night together and i can't
he drags me into a shop in the french quarter puts on a top hat says
he will marry
me right there   i explain to him the concept of manic pixie dream girl
because he's being too much   he says perhaps i am the
director   perhaps i've already written him as one
p tells me he can still smell me in our sheets but now my smell is
perfume & cigarettes

One night when I'm sleeping at M's, P texts me and says he would
consider having a threesome with M if only I weren't madly in love
with him—a prospect I never contemplated or mentioned, but now
I can't help but smile thinking about the completely impossible
scenario. In the sad and pleading and loving and angry texts and
emails P sends me while I'm at work or M's, he refers to M only by his
initial. I'm not sure if he thinks a letter is less powerful than a word or
more. *M, M* says playfully when I once call him by his initial, *means*
love in French. I don't repeat this to P.
The morning after M first arrived in New Orleans, P picked him up
and they drove to Panavision to check out the camera equipment for
the shoot together. They spent hours building the camera and testing
lenses and, after, P took him to get po'boys for lunch. P mentioned he

lived with me but, for some reason, didn't say we were together, as if we were roommates. M told P about a woman he'd recently broken up with, the director who'd recommended him to Lara for the job. When P got back to our apartment that afternoon, he told me M reminded him of one of his best friends. I agreed—there was something so familiar about him.

When I conjure the image of them laughing together, it's like a strange dream and I'm nostalgic for it. I want to be back in that feeling with them, even though I was never there, even though it was only a day.

Can't love just be fun? P asks me after the shoot is over, only hours after I dropped M off at the airport. We lie on the couch, and he holds me as I cry and still reek of M. He's asking me why this all has to be such a big deal, why I'm acting like the world is ending. I know I wouldn't have the same freedom with M as with P. M could never hear me say these words I say to P, *I have fallen in love with someone else,* and yet still hold me like this. P says he wants to know everything about me, even if everything about me now is obsessed with everything about M. He says he still wants to hear it, and for this I'm both disoriented and in awe of him. He doesn't see how my love for M could affect what still exists between us.

M says it's not possible to love two people at once. He says you always love one person more. I don't agree, I think. But I'm also not sure this can just be fun.

Your French Demon, my friend calls M the day after we ran into her at a dive bar, after watching him yell with the bartender about nothing, slam his fists on the jukebox, while I laughed at his indignant theatrics. Every time I go out with him, he gets into an argument with someone at the bar. He thinks Americans act strange, as if they're hiding something, as if they're scared of some deeper truth. When he's drinking, this drives him to frustration, even belligerent anger. *At some point,* I tell myself, *this will stop being cute, this will stop being funny.* I am trying my best to believe this is the kind of love that's fleeting (or maybe, rather, that what is fleeting is not significant).

When I drive him to the airport, M plays "Delta Dawn" on repeat.
He's played it many times over the past few days, since he first heard
the song when I played it in the car on the way to a shoot. I think he's
decided the song is about me, though for the first time he asks me
what it means. *"Delta Dawn" is a name?* he asks, pronouncing "dawn"
like "down." I contemplate this for the first time. *Delta Dawn*—it's
a name but it's also like the delta, *the land we are on, made by the
River,* and dawn, *like the time just before sunrise.* I translate the song
to him—I try to tell him the meaning of each sentence, attempting
to interpret the song's narrative. *It's about a woman who used to be
beautiful but is now deemed to be "past her prime" . . . too old,* I say,
*who people think is crazy because she's still waiting for a man who will
never come, waiting for a fantasy of a life that has passed her by, a life
that was maybe never possible because she wasn't given a chance.*
Because of M love has become a form of writing, making me choose
my words thoughtfully, making me think about our meaning. *What
is a "mansion in the sky"?* he asks. I tell him it's the fantasy. *Love is
always an act of translation,* I think.

Tanya Tucker was only thirteen years old when she became famous
for the song "Delta Dawn." I watch a grainy YouTube clip titled "tanya
tucker delta dawn live on hee haw aged 13 1973." She has blond hair
to her shoulders and a sweet little red dress that hangs to her upper
thigh, black tights underneath. When she sings she furrows her brow
and opens her mouth wide, revealing a gap between her two front
teeth. How is her small body capable of producing the sound of pure
longing, like she herself is forty-one-year-old Delta Dawn? As if, for
years, she has been waiting for a mysterious dark-haired man to
take her to his mansion in the sky, as if she could possibly know the
meaning of her own words.

They don't know the kind of bad trip I'm in, M says of his friends and
the other people he works with on commercial shoots, when he's back
in Paris. We talk on the phone for hours every few days. He sends
me a playlist with 154 songs, and I listen to it all the time. I miss him

more than I was hoping to. When I say *I hung out with a friend today*, he asks me to clarify the gender. He says the lack of context bothers him; he is used to the French way; he doesn't like ambiguity. He says he doesn't know whether or not to be jealous of this *friend*. I find this a bit absurd, considering M knows I'm still living with P. It's only 4:00 p.m. my time, but M is drunk on the phone and he says it's been so long since he's felt this way about a woman—*I'm sorry, I know you hate this, "a woman," I know in New Orleans you are . . . whatever the fuck but I don't care*—since he's felt this way about *anyone*, he concedes. And, somehow, even as I roll my eyes at how he expresses it, I hear myself echoing the sentiment.

I never took French in school, only Spanish. I thought people who took French were usually assholes, how so many of them would choose the less-spoken language because of what they deemed to be high culture. *C'est fou*, it's crazy. I look this up on Google Translate after M leaves. I say it under my breath. *C'est vrai*, it's true. I also look this up—he said this about us, about the way he feels about me. Soon, I get the two phrases confused in my mind.

hank's fried chicken sitting on the floor   fried bits falling to the
carpet   our last dinner together
that night he gets four dots tattooed   the four nights we spent in each
others' arms—
my dots, now they live on his inner bicep next to his *maman*
he wants me to get a tattoo for him but i can't   i want to so badly but
p will never take me
back
i realize i still want to keep this option open despite how i've acted
i drive m to the airport & we stop on decatur to go to molly's   a dark
bar open even at 10 in the morning   park illegally and get a ticket
$45 for a photobooth strip of us kissing
in front of the delta sign where i was supposed to pick him up we kiss
and i can't remember what our last words to each other are

we are underwater
when he walks away   toward the sliding airport doors   he does the
sign—his index finger to the middle of his lower lip like my lip ring—
the sign we said we'd do on set to secretly show we were thinking
about each other but never did
i get in the car sit in the driver's seat but cannot drive
i watch a woman on a bench who is smoking and watching me cry like
i'm her movie

On our last night together, M asked, *Is love enough?* He said he was
ashamed he'd thought this, but I didn't understand why, as it seemed
to me a fair question. We don't speak the same language, we come
from different places, cultures, we live our lives so far apart—I don't
even know what his real life looks like, and he is only a tourist in
mine. Is love enough to overcome what we cannot share, enough to
overcome an ocean? He said he wanted to speak English for me. But
when we speak of love, we are never speaking the same language. We
will never know what the word means in the mouth of another.
A few days after he left, while P was at work, I watched a short film
M directed. I read the English subtitles while the images spoke to
me beyond language. I wanted the film to be bad. I wanted to see his
faults more clearly so I could stop thinking about him, especially now
that he was back in Paris. *Fuck*, I thought, *the film is perfect.*
Could M ever read my writing? He said the only book he'd read in
English was *Animal Farm*, which he hated and barely understood.
Maybe it's a relief if he can't read what I write—it frees me to write
whatever I want about him. But it also makes me sad, because how
can he view me as a writer if he cannot read my words?
As we were eating a late dinner together one night after a shoot, M
asked me what I was writing for the low-residency writing program
I would soon graduate from. I tried to avoid the question, knowing
what I'd have to expose in talking about the project. But then I
thought, *fuck it*. I rarely had the chance to explain this for myself.
P had known before I'd even met him—someone had told him a

"Disney girl" had moved to New Orleans and had shown him a picture of me. With P, this weird fact was speaking for me before I ever opened my mouth. (And, later, speaking for me when I met P's family, who he told about my middle name before I met them— they are big fans, with annual passes to Disney World). P knew this about me as he initially pursued me, knew this before I ever knew he did. So I told M, *I'm writing essays about Disney, about my family.* I explained a bit more, about my relation and the writing, and he replied simply that he loved the movies so much when he was a kid. He told me with childlike wonder how he used to watch *Peter Pan* over and over again. He said this with no judgment, and I don't know why I was surprised. I asked him if the songs were translated and dubbed in French. *Yes, of course,* he said. I'd never considered this before. *J'ai des ailes, J'ai des ailes,* the chorus sings as Peter shows the kids how to fly up and over London, while little M was curled up on the floor in front of the small '90s television, riveted in front of these familiar images. A little boy, born in Geneva a year before I was to young parents of Spanish, German, French, and Moroccan descent, was excited by the *same* stories, was singing along to the *same* songs, as I was on the other side of the Atlantic, in front of a television screen in an apartment in Manhattan—so many children were, yet this still feels special, which perhaps is Disney's true magic.

The night after M flies back to Paris, P has to drive up to Shreveport in North Louisiana for work, and I'm alone for the first time in a month. I'm recklessly sentimental, and I drink bitter red wine from the fridge and watch *Jules and Jim* on the projector. I haven't seen the film in years, but I remember vaguely liking it and finding it funny. Now, I'm perplexed by my memory. The movie is not funny at all; it's actually pretty tragic. Well, I do like the part when the three of them are walking down a dark Paris street and the two men are talking about the importance of a woman's fidelity, so Catherine jumps into the river just to fuck with them.

You haven't known many women, but I've known plenty of men.
It averages out. We might make an honest couple.
One always feels guilty in a hotel room. I may not be very moral, but
I have no taste for secrecy.

I like Catherine. I identify with her. Everything Catherine does is in
the realm of possibility. She sleeps with two men, loves two men,
more. She can't be attached—she just won't be—even after she
marries, even after she becomes a mother. These identities don't
define her and don't alter her desires, and I respect her for this.
She follows her confusing heart, even when she hurts those around
her. Then, it gets to the end—the car, the bridge, the water—and
suddenly I recall how deeply betrayed I was by the film the first
time I watched it and again now. Am I supposed to identify with this
behavior: driving off a bridge with someone I love in the passenger
seat? After telling M about the concept of the manic pixie dream girl,
I looked it up again, to see if I explained it correctly. Wikipedia has
a comprehensive list of manic pixie dream girls: Sam from *Garden
State*, Faye from *Chungking Express*, Penny Lane from *Almost
Famous*, etc. Now, I notice Catherine from *Jules and Jim* is on it, one
of the first examples.

Sometimes, I feel like I am:
eyes   for seeing/reading
mind   for making sense of what I see/read
Otherwise I don't feel much like a body. I wonder how other people
feel their bodies. I wonder if this is odd, the way I'm in mine.

Alone, I get out of a movie around 9:00 p.m., and there's a WhatsApp
message waiting from M, from hours before: *Do you love me? Are you
my girl? I need to know / Sorry.* I get in P's car. I drive home, listening
to French songs from M's playlist but unable to respond to his message. My phone sits unlocked in the passenger seat beside me with
his words. The device has become a sentient presence, has become M.

I'm scared to look at it, but its light reflects off the windshield glass. In the movie version, perhaps I would drive off a bridge, into the Mississippi, phone/M in the passenger seat—would that prove I am no one's girl? Maybe I am that kind of person, manic, pixie, or maybe I have just written myself as one. I park down the street from our apartment. I pull the phone into my hands and respond slowly to M, forming some strange sentences that say I love him but I'm not really sure how to respond to the other question and maybe we should talk about it not over text. It's late his time, and I won't hear from him until my morning. I live on two time zones now, always aware of night somewhere else. I breathe. I check my email. There's an email from P, whom I will see upstairs, in our familiar living room, in only minutes. He says today he feels good about us but it ends:

> I guess i worry about what you and M talk about. There's a physics concept called the three body problem (and the name of that chinese sci fi book). Essentially when two objects orbit each other we can know exactly how they will move, but when you introduce a third object it causes chaos and there's no way to predict the motion of the objects.

I wonder how I can feel lonely when two people say they love me. When I talk to each of them so often there's hardly time to be alone. Is it because, now, I'm alone in my experience of love: I'm the only one who believes they love two?

There's also loneliness in dishonesty—that each of them thinks I love them the most and I can't bring myself to say I'm not sure this is true, these loves are not measurable, not comparable. They are both love, but they are so different they can exist simultaneously. For the most part, when I'm experiencing one, I'm not longing for the other; I am existing only in the moment of that particular love. P, of course, is the one I've loved for much longer. There is more certainty in this, in the years, but also more pain. Or there is certainty in the pain.

Sometimes I think I must be crazy. Sometimes—and maybe this is a remnant of my Catholic school upbringing—I wonder if I'm a "bad person," if bad people follow their desires, even when they hurt other people. If "good people" in relationships shove their desires into the dark edges of their hearts for the sake of those they love. If this is it, I know it's not possible for me to be a good person. I feel at home in myself when I am making the worst decisions.

Two weeks after M has gone, I'm reading Chantal Akerman's memoir *My Mother Laughs*, and it's so beautiful and sad and I don't know if it's the book that's making me feel this way or I just miss him. I lie on a patch of grass in the sun and read this small, perfect book and cry. *There is not only seeing in life there is also feeling. And sometimes feeling is worse*, she writes. In some ways, I am surprised a filmmaker would make this distinction—isn't watching a film a form of feeling? But I also agree with her: there is a difference, just as there is a difference between words—saying them/receiving them—and feelings, even if I have to remind myself of this all the time.
Today, I am so tired. I can barely move. I cannot work, I cannot write. I lie in the grass, under a huge oak tree, in the quiet field behind the Katrina memorial and beside a cemetery, a city of mausoleums, and stare at the sky, holding the book to my chest. But tomorrow, I will realize it. I will be sitting in a coffee shop, looking through all the sentences I've written in the past few years, asking myself for the hundredth time what the point of all this writing is, and then I will know. I have to leave. I have to move out, to be on my own. To buy a little truck again and get a cat again and write my stories and make my own life. Not "to be with" M, because that doesn't feel like freedom either—I don't want to be anyone's girl. I don't want to marry or have someone's kids. At least not now. A phrase will come back to me, something I wrote about P in my journal fairly early on in our relationship. *I feel most myself when we are falling apart.* I will go back to look at the rest of what I wrote almost six years ago: *I have never felt like a segment of a larger pair, and I've even readily fought this sensation, as if in the act of coupling I would lose something of myself as an individual.* I can't believe I'd forgotten the words that explained

this feeling, this feeling that never really left me. I will realize we've been together so long I'm not sure who I am anymore.

Tomorrow, I will realize the only way I can find my own ending, even if it will break our hearts, even if I still love him. I won't know if I have to leave because I'm scared or if I have to leave because I'm brave, but I will tell him anyway: I want to break up.

road trip

the awkward skinny bodies of palm trees   relating to each other with
planned precision
in groups   rarely alone
aging billboards for the fountain of youth   *Where Legend Meets History*
water mingling with land   long bridges over urban harbors
a car wash outside of st. augustine made to look like a
steamboat   almost life-sized   and a paddlewheel turning to scrub
cars clean
waterparks right next to the interstate   slides emerging from pirate
ships   discolored concrete volcanos   tubes curling endlessly around
each other like intricate hamster cages
p & i drive through florida

waiting

On our first day in Disney World, P and I wait for over an hour to go on a
new ride in the Animal Kingdom. In front of us are honeymooners—I can
tell from their matching pins that say "Happily Ever After"—who barely
speak to each other, staring at their phones for most of the slow march.
Behind us is a group of preteen girls, who sing together like they're at
summer camp "Body Like a Back Road," clapping to an imagined beat,
they know every curve like the backs of their hands . . . We move with

these bodies, the trail of us coiling in on itself again and again, deeper into the dark building, deeper underground. I know, conceptually, we're probably still above ground, but there are no windows and the space is designed to look like a cave and the realistic set decoration—fiberglass stalagmites, claustrophobic tunnels, a dripping sound emanating from a hidden speaker—is working its magic on me. Along the way are younger kids, restless, sitting on the floor or chasing each other. They refuse to obey the metal bars or sloping cave walls that guide us, delineating the shape of our collective, choreographed movements, a trail of ants boring deeper into our colony.

When my siblings and I came to Disney World when we were younger, our guide took us through the back entrances of the rides, so we never had to wait in the lines. We hardly ever entered any of the four parks through their main entrances at the front and, instead, always drove to one of the parking lots backstage, closest to whatever rides we wanted to go on. This allowed us to go to several parks in one day, only going on the rides we loved, even though we loved them purely out of habit. Like a favorite movie, we went on Pirates of the Caribbean and Thunder Mountain so many times we memorized every recorded line, every drop. When I was really young, I knew only that this was a privilege to be thankful for, a prize for having a famous middle name. As I got older, this routine became more uncomfortable—when I noticed the ride workers preventing other kids from getting on so we could, when I heard a child asking his mom pleadingly, *Why do they get to go?* Eventually, I found the only way I could enjoy going to Disney was if I brought a friend along so I could share this unearned right with someone who'd never experienced it. The last time I came to Disney World, I was nineteen and had brought a college friend I loved, unrequitedly.

Now, I'm twenty-seven, waiting in lines at Disney World for the first time in my life, realizing I don't actually know what any of the main entrances to the parks look like—P, who I've driven here from New Orleans with, playfully mocks me for this. Before, I didn't really understand the acute pain in that child's voice when he intoned, *Why do they get to go?* Before, I didn't know how waiting makes the ride more satisfying yet also amplifies the explosion of emptiness one feels when it so quickly comes to an end. How peculiar a day feels when so much of it is spent in anticipation, longing.

I wanted to find out what it would be like to come to Disney World again, and P humored me, agreeing to come here because of the adventure of the road trip, because I could get him into the park for free and, having come here a lot as a kid himself, I think he also secretly wanted a reason to come back. As soon as we drove into the park and I noticed every road sign was in the shape of a Mickey head, I felt overwhelmed by having asked P to come. We entered the hotel lobby, a hotel I'd never actually stayed at before, and yet I noticed it still somehow *smelled* like my childhood, like Disney. I didn't realize how intimate being here would feel, somehow more intimate than when P first met my parents years ago or saw me have a panic attack or, just three months earlier, told me he slept with A. More intimate than that recent night when he was out of town and she slept over with me. Though those moments were strange, painful, they were also realistically me, the part of me I recognized as myself and, therefore, P also knew. I didn't know how raw I'd become to him in a landscape I found at the same time dazzling and disturbing and all-too-familiar—how difficult it was to admit, to the person I care about most, that I was once at home in this identity, as a Disney.

yearbook

In our class's section of my high school yearbook, each graduating senior had their own informal black-and-white portrait printed above a series of humorous, personalized hypotheticals written by our friends, the best of which succeeded in illustrating the hypocrisies of our cultivated high school personas. In my photo, I'm laughing and looking down, dark, greasy hair falling in my face. I'm wearing a nose ring that's awkwardly oversized for my face, and I have my hands shoved into the pockets of a baggy naval jacket. When the yearbooks were printed and we excitedly picked them up from our class office, I quickly thumbed through the crisp pages, searching for my page. I grimaced at the photograph, which reminded me of how timid and insecure I must've appeared to the outside world, when I was trying so hard to look tough. But I enjoyed the hypotheticals my friends had written for me, which were, for the most part, cheekily disparaging. Because I was known for dressing sloppily, often wearing tights and T-shirts riddled with continuously growing moth holes, one of my hypotheticals was "Chachi will leave high school . . . with holes in her graduation gown."

My chest tightened at a more pointed jab, my "dream versus reality." It read: "Dream: vintage store, Reality: Disney store." A part of me wished I'd never told my friends my middle name. But I laughed—I was somewhat shocked by the perceptiveness of this silly joke and how it succeeded in so few words at encapsulating the dichotomy of my identity and how I wanted to be seen.

cafeteria

Our second day at Disney World, we arrive at the Magic Kingdom around noon and we're very hungry—almost immediately, we realize our mistake. So many people, sweating, hungry, hundreds of strollers lined up under signs for "Stroller Parking." The cheaper cafeteria option is brimming with humans, crying toddlers: an airport. We wait in a long line and pay too much for bad tacos, $14 a person for ground meat, and can't find a place to sit. How much have these families spent to be here? How much discomfort are they willing to tolerate?

I ask P these questions because he has become my frame of reference for what is "normal," as I try to understand the true experience of this place. I have to admit to him I've never been to any of the cafeteria restaurants here, because it was always easy for my family to make a reservation at a moment's notice at a sit-down restaurant, like the one inside Cinderella's Castle. My mom would pay with her "gold card," a credit card that worked only at Disney World and, there, it worked like magic as it was not connected to any bank account we knew of.

P and I sit at a dirty table beside a couple hunched over their sad meals, one of them bouncing a small, sleeping child in his lap. In telling P of my childhood version of Disney, an impossible place where everything was free, I'm realizing I've never told anyone this before. I recount to him how every time we went to Disney when we were young—as often as once a year before I was twelve—my sister and I would be ushered into a private room, where we'd be plopped into Mickey's lap, despite our tearful confusion regarding this oversized, overly enthusiastic mouse. His gloved hands containing us, we'd have our photo taken; though I think the point of these sessions was mainly to "meet" him. Saying it to P, I realize for the first time how the real people in those costumes, always some of the most ardent Disney fans, had probably been told of our relation—both funny and disturbing, the idea of Mickey greeting us children as if *we* were the famous ones. How ridiculous these words must sound as they exit my mouth. I'm reminded of a conversation I had with P's mom a year before. Over dinner she told me that when P was eight or nine, they'd seen a parade at Disney World that my grandpa Roy was in, riding in a vintage fire truck, waving to the crowd. *I was there, I was in that parade*, I gushed, though the memory had always felt like a dream. I had been there, in the fire truck with my cousins and my grandpa—we were instructed to wave at onlookers like we were washing a window, slowly side to side, up and down—the fact that this truly happened only confirmed by P's mom's memory of the event. I couldn't believe little P had been there in the crowd, though he doesn't remember it, watching the only parade I would participate in until moving to New Orleans many years later.

merchandise

We're standing at the edge of the large manmade lake at Epcot, and my gaze pauses mindlessly on a familiar silhouette, Cinderella's castle—it's our third day at Disney World and I've become numb to the ubiquity of these images—but, I come to realize, the castle is printed on a pale calf, on skin instead of clothing. A tattoo almost made more odd in this context, Disney-brand skin like something bought in one of those many stores but, of course, it couldn't have been. Next to Cinderella's castle, lower on the woman's calf, is a quote written in a font imitating Walt Disney's handwriting: a quote about magic and dreaming I can't quite make out before the woman shifts her position, moving the back of her leg out of my view.

On our first day here, I was overwhelmed by how many people were wearing Mickey and Minnie and Goofy ears, Cinderella and Elsa princess dresses, furry Lion King backpacks, Disney World T-shirts and pins, so many items I stopped being able to distinguish between them, the crowds a blur of merchandise. I'd forgotten how many people in the park participate in this massive costume party even though, when I was a kid, I did too.

When I was small, my parents dressed me as Belle, in a miniature version of her shiny yellow ball gown. Later, I dressed myself as a pirate, begging my mom for a plastic sword from the Pirates of the Caribbean gift shop, for small gemstones I could carry around in a little pouch and pretend they were treasure. When I learned how to feel embarrassed, just before puberty kicked in, donning Disney apparel suddenly seemed a creepy, redundant thing for me to do. Since then the only Disney-related items I've willingly owned are a small leather-banded Mickey watch I never wear and a T-shirt I bought at a thrift store. The worn gray shirt reads *Drunk* with a Disney-style *D* across the front. I wore it exclusively to high school parties, a 40 in hand, and hoped to be perceived as adept in irony and willing to make fun of myself. This is the same high school version of me who, when my female friends played the game "Never-Have-I-Ever," would say, provocatively but truthfully, "Never have I ever given a blowjob *not* in a public place" and watch those girls' eyes widen as I laughed, I thought, at them.

Walking around the different parks, I soon notice P and I don't look like most Disney park-goers. P is wearing very short cut-offs and a gold chain, is growing out his mullet, and has recently shaved his face, leaving behind a patchy mustache. He looks eccentric, though probably undefinably so to strangers, the level of sarcasm in his fashion sense perplexing even to me at times. I am probably equally confusing, especially at P's side, my shaved head, many piercings, sports bra or binder beneath my T-shirt. I don't see many people our age, except within the context of their families, and definitely not people who resemble my friends—punks, hipsters, and queer-looking people are a rare sight here. I know this is largely because of the cost-prohibitive tickets. Another reason for this is likely the cultural elitism of the spaces I often occupy, having been raised in Manhattan with a private school education and my subsequent life among filmmakers, writers, and other artists and intellectuals. Growing up, my friends couldn't mask their disgust when I talked about Disney World—why would they choose to spend tons of money just to vacation among throngs of *typical Americans*—so I stopped talking about it. In my high school, there were other kids with famous last names, kids whose parents were owners of well-known Manhattan establishments, pundits on CNN or MSNBC, or head editors at the *New York Times* or the *New Yorker*. To them Disney was lowbrow. To my artist friends later in life, Disney was too pervasive, too capitalist and, well, too expensive to be embraced even ironically.

Much like on Bourbon Street, groups at Disney World wear matching colored T-shirts to keep track of each other in crowds, shirts that say things like, "Disney Honeymoon Crew," "Disney Family Vacation," and "Most Magical Day Ever." We keep seeing dads around the parks with the same black T-shirt with a Mickey Mouse head next to the phrase "Most Expensive Day Ever."

I'm just now grasping the all-encompassing consumerism of this place, that this whole amusement park is just an elaborate mall. I know it's a little late to realize these things. My mom always told me the concept of "exiting through the gift shop" was invented by Walt, but I never quite understood how crucial this idea was to the experience of the park. This time around—now that I'm forced to idle among the merchandise, now that I'm not offered a back-door escape, now that I'm not with my mom and her gold card—it finally occurs to me everything in Disney World is a store, even the rides; every space is trying to sell you the illusion of happiness, a piece of the dream.

On a travel agency website called Vacation Kids, agent Sally Black does the math for the average cost of a family of four's vacation to Disney World in 2017. For six nights in a hotel (in Disney's "moderate" hotel category) and seven days of park passes ("the longer you stay, the more you save on admission") and food (on a family dining plan), she estimates the cost as $1,268 per person—$5,075 total for the four-person family, excluding travel expenses.[1] If you're flying, the national average for a round-trip plane ticket is $336, times four is another $1,344.[2] In 2017 the median American household income was $60,336.[3] A basic Disney experience including plane tickets, then, would be at least 10.6 percent of that yearly household income. And that's before you exit through the gift shop, your kids begging for their own plushy Simba for $32.99 or Tinker Bell costume for $44.99. For many families, making it to Disney is proof of success, a kind of validation—it's the American dream itself—so I understand why it's considered worth shelling out for. Disney, in turn, takes advantage of this reputation, carefully wielding its power by way of each enticement in the park and its inevitable price tag.

fireworks

P and I watch the fireworks light up the man-made lake at Epcot. Afterward, we run out of the park with the crowds and, despite the exhaustion of the day, everyone seems to be smiling, laughing, energized by the loud, colorful explosions still reverberating in our skulls. Suddenly, I feel enchanted by this place again, by the breadth of memories and connections people have with the park. How the different worlds and stories created by this company speak to so many disparate people and how I could never truly understand what it means to them. On the bus back to our hotel, I lean my head on P's shoulder, and I don't tell him what I'm thinking but I'm wishing I could see this place through his eyes.

I'm wishing I could understand what he sees, but the truth is I'm never really sure, his feelings always shrouded in ambiguity, a shyness I used to interpret as irony or cockiness. Even after he slept with A and we spent a few sloppy weeks "apart," I wasn't sure what he really wanted. He seemed to want to be with me, but I could garner this only through the magnetic pull that still existed between us and not through his words. At the time I asked him to write me a letter, not an apology, just something explaining why he did it. Really, I was hoping this letter would contain a confession of his love for me. I thought I was creating an opening for some kind of crazy fireworks show of love, like in the movies, like Disney—even though I knew P wasn't the kind of guy who did things like that, even though I'd previously told myself that was okay because I didn't need romantic theatrics. I prided myself on not needing them. He never wrote the letter in any form though and, over time, I forgot I asked him for one.

carousel

"You know, Walt loved the idea of progress, and he loved the American family. And he himself was probably as American as anyone could possibly be," states the off-screen robot narrator of the Carousel of Progress, a relic from the 1964 World's Fair, which hides in a largely ignored corner of the Magic Kingdom's "Tomorrowland." Forgetting myself I laugh loudly at this comment and the speaker's performative genuineness, and P looks at me, not quite as amused as I am. My laughter echoes uncomfortably among the otherwise silent audience, and the robot narrator continues his spiel, uninterrupted. When we were in our early teens, my sister and I loved this ride and always insisted on coming here because we found it so bizarre.

P and I sit in the dark, over-air-conditioned theater with only a few others, staring forward at a stage shrouded by a blue curtain. As the narrator speaks, our room begins to move and, as an audience, we rotate slowly around the circular center stage, through time, toward the first robotic tableau, where we see the robot narrator whose voice we've been hearing. He's sitting in a chair at the center of the stage, a white guy with brown hair and a mustache with a pipe in one hand and a newspaper in the other. He's wearing a formal-looking outfit with leather shoes and a red tie, paired with a green smoking jacket since he's at home. We watch his stilted motions as he moves his arms and sings "There's a Great Big Beautiful Tomorrow."

A young employee died on this ride in the '70s, crushed to death between a rotating wall and the nonmoving stage wall. I'm not sure where I heard this, but it's a difficult fact to ignore here. It feels like there should be some kind of memorial to her in one of the parks but, of course, there's not, as the company goes to great lengths to cover up any deaths that occur on company property and would much prefer everyone forget that awful things happen, ~~even~~ *especially* at Disney.

The theater comes to a stop in front of the first tableau, and the song ends. The narrator robot, the father of the family, explains that it's the turn of the century and tells us about all the newfangled technology in his home. Each device he mentions comes to life with his acknowledgement of it. The ice box opens and closes; the gas lamps turn off and on. I always liked this part, how the stage set talks back to the robot, how the space itself feels so eerily alive. Soon, an opaque scrim on the left side of the stage becomes transparent, and through it we can see the mother robot and the little daughter robot doing laundry. The mother robot marvels at their new washing system, which takes only five hours as opposed to the two days it used to take her to do the laundry. Now she has more time for her other household chores: *Well, ovens just don't clean themselves, you know, dear.* The scrim of the diorama becomes opaque again, and a screen on the right side of the stage reveals the little boy robot, Jimmy, in his father's office, gazing into a stereoscope.

JIMMY

Wowee! Look at that!

FATHER

Now James, I thought I told you to ask my permission
before using my new stereoscope. That's not a toy you
know!

JIMMY

Ooh-la-la! So that's Little Egypt doing the hoochie-
koochie, eh Dad?

FATHER

Isn't she a knockout? She's the star of the new World's
Fair in St. Louis, and—(*clears throat*) now you put that
away before your mother finds it.[4]

I forgot how corny this ride is, how comically dated the characters are,
though this is partially what my sister and I found so amusing about
the attraction. Hearing it now, there's something familiar about the
dialogue—it's a sitcom, the same script. The stereoscope with the image
of the exoticized belly dancer, "Little Egypt" as she's called, is like an
antiquated *Playboy* magazine. I'm reminded of the more sinister aspects
of this ride's corniness, which seem all the more palpable in the age of
"Make America Great Again." I've since learned how nostalgia can be used
as a harmful tool, to divide, to maintain power through hate. I don't think
I could have seen it as clearly as a teenager, when this ride was simply
weird to me and I couldn't pinpoint exactly why I found it so outrageous.
I didn't know what I know now: that Walt's vision of the ideal American
family—a family that is, without question, white and heteronormative
and adheres to these predictable dynamics—was not outrageous; it was
a vision shared by many members of this country and permeates our
society so many years after the ride's inception. And, significantly, Walt
wanted this ideal family to persist into the future, to remain unchanged.

The ride continues, and the seated audience rotates around the stage to the next tableau, which takes place twenty or so years later. Again, as we move, the robots gesture awkwardly with their arms and sing the theme song about how it all started with a man having a dream.

We move through time, yet the family remains the same. The narrator is the same, his wife, his daughter, his young son—the setting is different but the characters and the way they interact with each other remain frozen in time. The last tableau, which is set in some unnamed future time period but is basically the '90s, is the only one in which we see any variation in the family dynamics. It's the only tableau in which the narrator, the father robot, is standing and is in the kitchen cooking while the mother is sitting at a computer. A little on the nose, perhaps, but at least they tried. This tableau, however, is the only one entirely invented after Walt's death and, therefore, the only one not within his vision.

Throughout Disney World we are constantly reminded of Walt's obsession with progress, his *dedication to innovation*. It's a concept of progress, however, that's limited to technology, to consumerism. "Spaceship Earth," the ride that's housed in the big golf ball–like structure at Epcot, is essentially a large-scale version of the Carousel of Progress. Small plastic cars, attached to each other like a train, slowly move ridegoers from the beginning of time to present, detailing "all" of humans' technological and communication innovations, from cave paintings to the invention of the computer. Epcot was once envisioned by Walt to be a utopian community of the future, an actual city that would exist on the Disney World property near Orlando. EPCOT stands for Experimental Prototype Community of Tomorrow, but Walt's original dream for this urban community was ultimately abandoned after his death, deemed too risky a venture. Apparently, Walt's brother, my great-grandfather Roy O., tried to save the project, even coming out of retirement to do so. He couldn't convince the board, however, that city planning was something the Disney company had any business doing.

In a promotional film about Disney World from 1966, Walt discusses the plans for the new property, swampland in Florida twice the area of Manhattan. He talks about the new parks they're constructing and his plans for the innovative city of EPCOT. He says that, with EPCOT, he aims to find solutions to the "problems of our cities"—the only way to create this kind of utopian community, he says, is to start completely from scratch.[5] A narrator brings us through the wheellike layout of EPCOT, as animations illustrate how the inhabitants will use lines of transportation that branch out from the center like spokes. I'm intrigued by Walt's serious commitment to public transportation, which would have been a significant feature of the community. The narrator says families would only ever have to use their cars on the weekends, for trips out of the city. At the center of the wheel is the "area of business and commerce," where members of the community go to both work and consume. The narrator marvels at how the center will be completely enclosed and climate controlled, mimicking ideal weather conditions. The center of Walt's EPCOT, the place he believes to be the heart of the community, is essentially a huge mall. Standing in front of a wall papered with huge scale drawings for EPCOT, Walt explains that his city's main goal will be to "showcase to the world the ingenuity of American free enterprise."

The film doesn't talk in depth about who the members of this new community will be, but it's clear the city is geared toward "typical American families." People, I'm guessing, who look and act like the robots on the Carousel of Progress.

Even though it's so distinctly a family destination, I spend our days drifting around Disney World never once considering a future version of P and myself pushing our way through the park with strollers or tugging small, sticky hands. I've never really thought about the possibility of us becoming a "typical American family." We only talked about kids or, rather, not having them, a few times earlier on in our relationship—P was wary of the whole thing, his parents having had him when they were teenagers and, later, his younger sister giving birth to her daughter when she was still in high school. To P, parenting seemed like a nondecision, a difficult lifestyle that only happened by accident, or at least that's what he thought when I met him. (And maybe his aversion to kids also had something to do with being raised to believe he would get another life, another chance, and an infinite one at that—even if he didn't believe anymore, I think an element of this stuck with him, and this Jehovah's Witness concept of our current life being a trial run contributed to his approach to love, to his general indecisiveness.) I too was still locked into the stubborn belief system I'd adhered to when we met, when I was twenty-two. I'd always declared, proudly, that I didn't want kids. I thought that having kids meant being *normal*, like my parents, and though my upbringing was, for the most part, a happy one, I didn't want to be locked into this dreadfully heteronormative existence, especially as a "woman" with a "man." Reproduction seemed like a surefire way to get stuck in all the worst realities of those gender roles—after all, my dad did end up cheating and my mom feeling betrayed. At twenty-two my imagination wasn't strong enough to picture an atypical existence with kids, though I've now seen many examples. So as I approach my thirties, I find myself still clinging to the part of me that doesn't want to grow up, that doesn't want to make a real decision about it, that would rather just say *fuck that* like the badass I wish I were. Plus, in all honesty, I feel pretty neutral about kids themselves, especially babies—looking at those squishy beings doesn't turn me into goo or anything, like some of my peers. Perhaps, though, I don't want to have a real opinion on the matter because it requires thinking deeply about the future. Then I would have to admit, to myself at least, that even when we're happy, I never picture P's and my future selves.

my imagination

Years ago I heard someone joke about how ridiculous it is that Minnie is just Mickey with eyelashes and a bow—how the two characters are drawn exactly the same except for these small details, how even in cartoon form woman is a derivative of man. At the time, I agreed with the sentiment. But now, I wonder what it really is that makes Mickey a "man" to begin with. The fact that he wears pants? The way he holds himself? Who he *is*?

My experience of being a woman is not dissimilar to Minnie's—when I am presenting as a woman, I feel like Mickey wearing an oversized, flashy bow and fake eyelashes. I feel the same as I did before but with these simple aesthetic additions.

As I walk around Disney World, I wonder if all these people come here, despite the many shitty aspects of the experience, because they can become imagined versions of themselves, who are still capable of childlike amazement. Even though they're not wearing costumes like their children, perhaps for some adults simply being here is a form of a costume, of fantasy—like all those grownups I see on Mardi Gras day with elaborate headdresses and suits made of sequins and masks of papier-mâché, outfits they've spent months creating, just to wear on this one day, just to feel like kids again.

I wonder if P will see me as I want to be seen, like I was when I was a kid, like the little boy/girl I still am. If he will call me *they* if I really ask him to, instead of just posing it to him as a hypothetical, which he never responds to the right way, so how can I really insist on it? I'm not even sure if for me it's about a pronoun, a word wanting to express something potentially inexpressible—yet somehow I need him to see.

dedication

A bronze plaque near the entrance of the Magic Kingdom reads:

> Walt Disney World is a tribute to the philosophy and life of Walter Elias Disney . . . and to the talents, the dedication and the loyalty of the entire Disney organization that made Walt Disney's dream come true. May Walt Disney World bring Joy and Inspiration and New Knowledge to all who come to this happy place . . . a Magic Kingdom where the

young at heart of all ages can laugh and play and learn—together.
Dedicated this 25th day of October, 1971 *Roy O. Disney*

Walt died before Disney World was finished, so Roy O., my great-grandfather, was the one to dedicate the park. Near the plaque is a life-sized metal statue of Roy O. sitting on a bench with Minnie Mouse. He's holding her hand and smiling at her. When P and I find the statue, a small girl dressed as Minnie is sitting on the bench beside the statues, and her mom is taking pictures. We wait behind her mom, beside the stroller, awkwardly, for the photo shoot to come to an end. The little girl puts her arm around Minnie's shoulder, leaning toward the statue lovingly as if she expects her to come to life.

When they're finished I take the little girl's place on the bench and, with his phone, P takes a few pictures of me with the metal version of my great-grandpa. He died in December of 1971, very soon after the dedication of Disney World, so I never met him in real life. My mom speaks fondly of him and always insists, with a mischievous smile, she was his favorite grandkid. I rest my elbow on the cool surface of Minnie's head, inspecting the sculpted wrinkles of Roy's old face. What would this man have thought of me, his kin? Even my hardcore feminist mom occasionally has a difficult time with my presentation—the horror in her face the first time she saw my shorn skull, her furrowed brow when she catches sight of my armpit hair, a particularly sloppy outfit, or another tattoo—I don't know if my great-grandfather could've ultimately gotten past these aspects of my body the way she does. I think about who I imagine myself to be, a self sometimes neither girl nor boy (sometimes one or the other or both), and I know this does not fit within the Disney imagination. For one last photo, I sit on the hard metal of Roy's lap, laughing—P tells me I'm weird and rolls his eyes but keeps snapping photos with a smile, so I know he thinks it's cute. I jump up from the metal lap of my relative and wrap my arms around the real, warm torso of P. He bends over, kissing me on the top of my fuzzy skull. I'm so glad he agreed to come here with me.

Walt's presence is felt so vividly in Disney World in part because of my great-grandfather. My mom has told me how important it was to Roy the company be called the "Walt Disney Company," instead of its original name, "Disney Brothers Cartoon Studio," to emphasize his younger brother's creative vision. In (Walt) Disney World, one is constantly reminded of this vision, of the mythical man who dreamed this place into existence. The voice-over narration on the "people-mover" ride in Tomorrowland, as well as on the train that encircles the Magic Kingdom, talks about the park as a place of the imagination, specifically Walt's. In these types of narrations, there is always an insistence on the impressive scope of Walt's imagination, which seems to have been something vast and irrepressible. Walt as a dreamer, a creator, an innovator, an artist—at least, that's how they sell him to us. At the end of Main Street in the Magic Kingdom, right in front of Cinderella's castle, there's a statue of Walt. He's standing beside Mickey, his left hand grasping Mickey's gloved hand, the other raised, waving to a nonexistent crowd.

morocco

On our last day, P and I go to Epcot and, in the afternoon, we slip tiny squares of paper from my fanny pack onto our tongues—acid that a friend had left over from Mardi Gras, we'd brought it to Florida for this purpose—but it doesn't work at all, and somehow only makes us feel headachy and then impossibly tired. We wander through the different countries as the sun goes down and, after accepting the reality of the disappointing drugs, decide to get drunk instead. We buy a bottle of red wine with a screw-top in France and store it in P's backpack. In Morocco we buy one cup of wine and ask for an extra cup, which one of the fez-capped guys at the counter—who appears to be only a teenager with his sparse mustache—fills for free. P tries to give him $5, handing the bill straight to him since there's no tip jar, but he looks back at his coworkers and an older-looking manager and refuses the money with a vehemence P and I later agree is unnerving. In the empty, intricately tiled courtyard behind the Morocco restaurant, we down our plastic cups of wine beside a quiet fountain. We crack open the French bottle, filling our cups again to the brim. For the rest of the evening, we walk in circles around the world showcase, drinking wine and going into every single gift shop but not buying a thing.

red tide

When we leave Disney World the next morning, driving north on the interstate out of Orlando, I find myself viewing all infrastructure in relation to Disney. Partially, my inclination toward comparison is because Disney's influence has bled over onto almost all tourism-related businesses in Northern Florida. It's as if every Florida hotel, every waterpark, every gas station is trying to trick you into thinking it's somehow related to Disney and, in this sense, everything has a counterfeit vibe.

There's a familiar disappointment in leaving Disney, and I'm surprised I still feel it despite my age, despite all my cynicism about the place—the feeling that the outside world cannot live up to Disney. Similar to the days after an acid trip (a real one, not like our attempt at Epcot), once the excitement of the experience has worn off, the world just seems duller, not so full of intense and surprising associations. Driving through Florida we are quickly immersed back in America, and not America of the imagination, but America of beige strip malls and car dealerships and identical subdivisions with names that always sound the same. In the outside world, a building is simply a building, a structure for humans to exist inside of, and not a place to house some elaborate fantasy.

P and I drive to the Gulf, to Florida's armpit, in the hopes of swimming in blue water before reaching the brown-water beaches closer to Louisiana, the sediment of the Mississippi River darkening the water all the way to the short strip of Alabama coast. Nearing the Gulf, we stop at a massive flea market in an open-air warehouse. We walk through makeshift booths with dusty army equipment, cardboard boxes of comic books, Confederate flags, rusted jewelry, concealed-carry handbags, an empanada truck, where we get empanadas. We drive on, hoping to get to the campsite before sunset so we can set up our tent. P and I, a man and sort of woman, camping—perhaps some version of the American dream Walt envisioned, like those theoretical weekend automobile trips taken by members of the Experimental Prototype Community of Tomorrow.

We arrive at a state park near Destin and get a campsite but soon learn from a park ranger the nearby beaches are currently not swimmable. Apparently, red tide is afflicting much of the east and west coasts of Florida, and the beaches are covered in algae and dead fish—the fetid smell of their carcasses hangs in the air, we realize, even at our campsite. We're overheated because it's been so hot all day and we can't swim. As it gets dark, we make pasta on our camping stove and try to ignore the smell.

Unable to fall asleep just yet and not sure what to do with ourselves, we leave our tent and drive into Destin to walk around. There's a fancy, fake-looking town square, where little kids are chasing each other in the grass and preteens are walking around in groups and eyeing each other predatorily. Parents sit outside of low-lit restaurants, wearing white and drinking large glasses of wine. Everyone has that night-beach-vacation look, tanned and showered, though none of them could've been swimming in the actual ocean today. Like at Disney World, P and I seem to be the only people around who do not belong to a more "fully realized" family unit. We sit in the itchy grass and people-watch and, seeing the small girls in their tight tank tops, with overdone makeup and straightened hair, I find myself so glad I'm no longer a preteen. I ask P if he gets sad when he leaves Disney, and he laughs and says he did when he was a kid, but not anymore.

we should kiss between our sigh

In a small hotel in Abita Springs, the town where he grew up, P gets into the bathtub with me. Warm water sloshes onto the floor, making space for our bodies. It's late November. We are broken up but we are not. Somehow we're more in love than ever. *Our breakup tour*, we jokingly call it. In a few weeks, I will see M again. We are drunk, we are kissing, reduced to our wetness. P pulls my face backward under the surface, and I reemerge coughing-laughing, water in my nose. I do the same to him so he knows what it feels like. He agrees it does not feel good. Soon, we dry ourselves. We stumble into a bed that is not our own and take photos of each other with my Nikon even though we know there's not enough light—the photos probably won't come out when we take them to be developed; the images will be suspended only in our minds. Even as it unfolds, the memory of us is already fading.

At the very beginning of our relationship, I texted P a quote from a book I was reading at the time, *The Price of Salt* by Patricia Highsmith: *But when they kissed goodnight in bed, Therese felt their sudden release, that leap of response in both of them, as if their bodies were of some materials which put together inevitably created desire.* The words immediately made me think of him. They made me think of how I wanted to write of this love. And also how I'd always wished someone would write about me.

Two months after the October shoot with M, the director, Lara, and I
drive over two hours north from New Orleans to look for a huge cypress
tree our friend told us about, an old growth tree at Cat Island Reserve.
The reserve has been closed for half the year, the Mississippi River over-
flowing and making the roads impassable, which is why we weren't able
to film there with M as we hoped. When we finally get to Cat Island, I'm
driving and one of M's songs is playing, "A la folie" by Juliette Armanet.
It's raining. I follow a sign with an arrow pointing to the reserve and
turn onto a dirt road. We wind down muddy roads, descending deeper
into thick forest that doesn't look like the Louisiana I'm familiar with.
We cross a flat cement bridge over a small brown river and, on the other
side, I start to feel the car slipping. I'm not sure if it's in my mind. I ask
Lara how far we have to go according to her phone, and the car keeps
sliding across the road so I stop. We get out and, sure enough, we're
sinking. The road is basically river—how could we forget we live in a
place where these boundaries barely exist? It's been so long since M
left, since I put my fingers through his dark, dense hair. I am starting
to slip, to forget. I'm starting to wonder if it's crazy to see him again. He
wants me to meet him in New York, the weekend before I was planning
to spend time in the city with my family for Christmas. Days before, he
told me not to kill him but he'd booked a hotel room in Times Square.
Laughing, he said he wants me to be a tourist in my hometown with him.
I want to, but I'm scared. This doesn't feel like reality. I've been so tired
lately. Lara and I push mud off the tires with sticks. I walk while Lara
slowly backs the car up so we can park it on more certain ground and
look for the tree on foot. We walk through cold rain, for thirty minutes,
to the end of the muddy road. We don't find the tree.

i love falling in love
what is wrong with me
i've always thought it was because i watched too many romantic
comedies growing up
but now I'm wondering
if it's actually because i watched too many disney movies

what a horrifying thought   i've been brainwashed
my family created something that could brainwash
but that story was always about the embrace
not the falling
apart
about the beauty of the castle   love as the
construction   infrastructure built
not the intricate and unknowable swamp buried beneath

In one of his lyric essays in *The Book of Delights*, Ross Gay talks about a student of his who says she believes that in each body, each soul, is a wilderness. And, further, she suggests these wildernesses inside us could be joined. Gay is blown away by this concept, and he wonders if the wilderness we each contain has something to do with our sorrow—the unique sorrow each person carries. Gay writes, *Is sorrow the true wild? / And if it is—and if we join them—your wild to mine—what's that? / For joining, too, is a kind of annihilation. / What if we joined our sorrows, I'm saying. / I'm saying: What if that is joy?*

Would you like to marry a Frenchman? the British Alan Squier (Leslie Howard), pipe in his hand, asks the young Gabby Maple (Bette Davis) in the 1936 black-and-white film *The Petrified Forest*. I went to the Petrified Forest National Park recently with P when we road-tripped from New Orleans to California. I took a black-and-white photo of the layered canyons between his long legs. Even if I hadn't been to the movie's namesake, I would be able to tell the film was shot not in Arizona but on a soundstage, tumbleweeds pushed across the landscape by someone on the edge of the frame at decided intervals. In the film Gabby has been confessing to Alan, a British drifter, a stranger passing through, her dream of someday moving far away from the desert. She wants to go to Bourges, France, where her mom was from. They are standing on the roof of the roadside diner where Gabby works, her dad's business in the middle of nowhere, Arizona, when he asks her if matrimony is the reason she has her sights set on France.

Oh, I don't want to ever marry.

No?

I want to be always free.

Gabby is holding several of her paintings of the desert under one arm—all her life, she's kept her art a secret but, finding something familiar in a foreigner, she shows her paintings to Alan. She tells him she wants to go to France because there are art schools over there, but she knows it's an impossible dream; how will she ever get the money to go? The way Bette Davis says *Bourges* with her American accent, making it into two syllables, reminds me of how I clumsily pronounce French words and am always surprised when M finds this endearing. I too want to be always free, and I wonder if this is selfish. Alan tells Gabby that to be a great artist she has to get used to being a colossal egotist; she has to get used to being selfish to the core.

I'm a player, I just got it like that, I say to P, partially joking. I pull the hood of my sweatshirt over my nearly bald head as I say it. We're in a dark, dirty restaurant in the Quarter. We're talking about how, for the first six months we were hooking up, I was having sex with multiple other people and P wasn't. *You knew what you signed up for from the beginning,* I say, pushing it further, even though he looks sad, even though soon I will leave to see M in New York. But for some reason I can't stop myself. I always feel like a playful little boy in my hoodie. This summer I was wearing the hoodie, and a bartender actually did think I was a little boy. She thought P was my dad. *He can't sit at the bar,* she said to P, gesturing at me. When I try to think of classic women players, the first one that comes to mind is Mae West. I love how she reduces Cary Grant to a child—it's almost unnerving to see his lanky body in her presence; he's suddenly just so pathetic. *Oh you could be had,* she tells him, turning up the stairs in a sparkling dress that's almost a part of her; it could be her skin.

In December my fancy older neighbors across the street host a party almost every night of the week. How do they have the energy, when I can barely finish a movie without falling asleep? Tonight, they're all piled out on the balcony wearing Santa hats and carrying huge glasses of wine and well-dressed babies. I eat alone on my balcony in full view of the party so they might see me and reflect on how all Christmas music is, at its heart, deeply depressing. When I'm done with dinner, I watch a German movie I've never seen before, Maren Ade's *Everyone Else*, on the projector. For once I don't fall asleep, because I'm mesmerized. The film is about a couple, Gitti and Chris, vacationing at Chris's mother's house in Sardinia. Their relationship is kind of fucked up but in an ambiguous, banal way that strikes me as familiar. Gitti, a publicist for a rock band, is a little wilder, weirder, than Chris and wants to go out and make new friends on the island while Chris prefers to stay inside, scared of running into a fellow architect he knows is there on vacation and whom he doesn't really like. One night they're getting ready for bed and Gitti, standing over the bed, short hair slightly mussed, admits, *Sometimes I want so badly to be different for you.* When Chris asks her how she would want to be, Gitti says she pictures him with other women, women they pass on the street who are completely unlike her, and this makes her think she would make him happier if she were different. But the saddest thought, she explains, is that being different would be the only way she could get to know Chris in another manner. The only thing that would allow him to relate to her differently. Chris confesses he has these thoughts too sometimes: *I always think I'm too boring for you.* He says, when he first met her, he always pictured walking into a room where she was and she'd say something to him and he'd just jump out of a window.

I find myself googling absurd phrases such as *is it possible to fall in love too much?* and scrolling around websites like "eHarmony Advice," "Psychology Today," and "The Date Mix." The articles are mainly about loving *one* partner too much. They advise their reader not to smother their partner, not to scare them away. I don't, however, find what I'm looking for: I don't find any articles about falling in love with too many people at one time. Though one website, called "Inspiring Tips," says:

If you love someone too much, your reasoning might be clouded. It will be difficult to see what's right or wrong. For example, you might come to a point in your relationship where you will find emotional and physical abuse okay just because you love your partner. You might even find it acceptable if your partner gets a third party as long as he or she keeps a relationship with you. Being blind because of excessive love can warp your reasoning.

The passage disturbs me. I want to ask whoever wrote it, *Is there a version of love where your reasoning remains intact, unwarped?* I know I would look crazy for even posing the question. But what is love if not distortion or, at least, some form of disorientation?

In mid-December, P drives to Mississippi to stay with a friend because we are trying harder to be on a break or broken up or whatever this is—he insists that he's the one who should move out and he's had no luck at finding a new place to move into, so we keep sleeping together and getting closer and closer, and it's not what I was imagining when I said *break up* at all. P emails me from Mississippi:

> Just remembered you last night at port of call looking so cute proclaiming youre a player. Wish i was back in that moment

> Looking back I played upset. Intentionally making my face upset and allowing my emotions to follow. Feeling I should have been upset but actually just thinking how lucky I was to be/have been with you. The cutest player

A year and a half ago, just after P first slept with A, I sent him Prince's "When You Were Mine." I listened to it over and over again during that summer as I biked around New Orleans, pondering what would happen to us. Now, I listen to it again, singing along, laughing sadly at its relevance: how you can know that your person is going with someone else and somehow not care, how you can even love that person more than you did when they were yours.

one night   i find myself messaging m while p runs his palm across my back
suddenly   i remember: texting p one morning while lying next to m in bed
has he texted me from a bed with her?
how could it possibly still hurt to think that?
when i've done what i have
in *love in the time of cholera* florentino ariza realizes he's capable of loving multiple people at
the same time   feeling the same care   the same anguish for each
my heart has more rooms than a whorehouse
he thinks with anger

In *The Petrified Forest*, Alan ends up falling completely in love with Gabby—this becomes clear when, later in the film, he secretly asks notorious gangster Duke Mantee (Humphrey Bogart) if he will kill him so Gabby can use his life insurance to move to France and pursue her dream of being an artist. *I want to show her that I believe in her, and how else can I do it? Living, I'm worth nothing to her,* Alan says. In the final scene, Gabby holds Alan, shot dead as promised, in her arms. I'm so moved by Alan, by his wildness in love—and also surprised by this kind of love story, one that fades out on an embrace the audience knows only Gabby will walk away from. She'll walk away and into a different kind of love story, one with her art.

on the plane about to land in the city where i grew up   amazed how calm i feel in this moment
even though i still love p
even though i am watching us descend toward that familiar skyline
and listening to *deeper than the holler*
it's so cheesy but on more than one occasion this song has led me to imagine
dancing with p (he hardly ever dances)
even, a wedding

which is the hardest truth for me to admit
i also believe in fairytales   like my mom
i enjoy believing in them
my love is stronger than the River
and yet i know i still want to do this
soon i will be in room 4209 with m
looking over times square glowing red
how can i do this   to both of them
but this is who i am: a person capable of so many contradictory
emotions i can hardly keep track

In her essay "Fucking like a Housewife," Jamie Hood writes, *My god. I know I could love any man if I were to focus my attention on him long enough.* Yes, I say, how awfully true. She continues, *I can't help myself. I want to be undone by love. I would give my whole life for this.* I am thankful for her words—how ashamed I've felt to share in this passion for much of my life. In her admission I find refuge. I too have lived to be undone; though, sometimes, for the experience of love just as much as the experience of commemorating the promise, the pain, of that love in writing. When love falls apart, I'm left with the words; I own them; they are my only constant.

For the four days just before Christmas, room 4209 on the 42nd floor of the Sheraton Times Square is our mansion in the sky. More air than property, room 4209 is the dream space where M and I live together. I don't tell my family or any of my friends who live in New York that I'm there and all my New Orleans friends know I'm gone, so no one reaches out to me. For the first time in years, P does not text or call or email. I exist only in this room with M. *L'écriture c'est le cœur qui éclate en silence.* It's morning and we're sitting on the bed, and M gives me a present, a framed white page with just these words and a 2 at the top, like a chapter heading. He carefully ripped out one of the title pages of a book by Christian Bobin he was reading as it reminded him of me. I think he's a little embarrassed by the gesture now, bringing the page to be professionally framed, wrapping it carefully, and transporting it across the ocean. Or maybe I'm just embarrassed, never knowing how to respond to gifts, especially one so thoughtful. He asks me to try to translate, and I feel so bad when I stare at the page and the letters do not come together to form meaning. Surprised when I don't get it, he translates for me: *Writing is the heart that bursts in silence . . . explodes in silence.* That day we walk around MOMA for hours and hours. We look at the art, we look at each other. M makes me see the world more lyrically. I want to write it all down—all the meaningless things I now notice, which suddenly seem so important. With M every coincidence carries a whole life within it, like each line in a poem: both significant and weightless, a feeling that could just fly away in a draft of air if you don't catch it with words. M makes falling in love into a poem I want to write over and over again.

I've always had a hard time putting into writing why I love P. I always thought this was because it was a feeling of wholeness beyond words. He is my best friend. The person I want to talk to about everything, who it made sense to sleep next to every night. Who I grew up with. But his most romantic act was the most surprising: when he agreed to separate, when he said it was the right decision, even though we were lying on the floor of our apartment, holding each other, crying, like the hardwood floor was the River, like we were being pulled apart by the current.

on the lower east side the tattoo guy asks if we are love birds   i say
something like that
m says to me yes we are birds   we are tornados   we are things that
fly: our tattoo is an abstracted
flight map m drew with ballpoint pen on a napkin in the dark bar we
were in minutes before
italy to new orleans the tattoo guy says *that's cute*
we smile and don't correct him as he puts needle to skin
a thread pulling us together across the ocean like   a submarine
communications cable

transmitting all our whatsapp messages under the sea
in new york   m is a form of time travel through my own life
i hear the sounds of sirens on buildings for the first time because he
shows me how to
i feel free again   like i only did when i was a child
with m i remember with my body all of these old versions of myself
when i was younger in times square, in central park, chinatown,
st. marks
i am becoming manhattan again
sometimes i forget i grew up on an island

In November, a few weeks after M returned to Paris after the shoot, one
of P's friends was having a birthday party at a karaoke place. P refused
to go. He wanted to stay in our dark bedroom by himself. I went, to give
him space, even though they're more his friends than mine. They'd gotten a private room for the party, and everyone was singing '90s songs
together, sharing the mics—the songs we grew up with, Destiny's Child,
Blink 182, Say Anything, Britney. I drunkenly typed "Delta Dawn" in as
a request, and when it finally came on, I stood alone with the mic on the
small stage, unsure what my plan was or why I'd decided to interrupt
the energy of the party for an inside joke with myself. First, I sang the
song normally, a slight twang in my voice, imitating how Tanya Tucker
politely shifts her hips as she dances. The others in the room didn't
seem to know the song, but they watched me expectantly, grinning,
like I was supposed to really perform it. I started to feel like I was not
myself anymore or like I was a wilder version. I was swirling around
someone but, this time, it was just myself, just the words of the song.
As I sang the chorus, I fell to my knees, my voice increasing in volume,
I pretended to do an interpretive dance, I rolled around on the floor. My
small audience whooped, laughing, surprised. I got up, I screamed the
song into the microphone, I screamed the song like I was really losing
it and jumped off the stage and got in people's faces, pushing them, like
it was a punk song, and they smilingly pushed back. Toward the end of
Maren Ade's *Everyone Else*, Gitti jumps out the second-story window of

the house where they're staying in Sardinia, just launches herself out of the open window like it's nothing. Chris finds her on the grass—she's only slightly hurt, having landed on her ass on the soft ground—and they fuck right there in the yard. He didn't see her jump out the window, and she doesn't tell him she did it. Like a tree falling in the woods, a heart exploding in silence. I scream, *Delta Dawn, What's that flower you have on, could it be a faded rose from days gone by?* And now I'm falling from a window, alone. I'm thankful to own this action—neither P nor M there to see me.

my mom takes a goldfish in her hand   it falls to the ground and she picks it back up
she peels back the grated top of the small aquarium   throws it in
and we watch in horror as the turtle chases the fish in circles and finally catches it in its jaws
i can't believe m is here   in my mom's house   on his last night in new york   my whole family together like a month ago at thanksgiving but p was there that time
my parents   still trying to be friends   my three siblings
no one asks m where he's from or how I met him   i guess that's fine since i confessed only an hour before that i was already in nyc with this new person
at dinner i tell them about a girl i met recently who went skydiving two years ago
the instructor she was attached to died of a heart attack   mid-fall
she didn't have a parachute   yet somehow survived   the impact taken by his body below hers
later   my sister and brothers play piano and sing
m asks if he can take a turn at the piano   plays the first song he ever sent me on whatsapp   "la ritournelle"   by sébastien tellier
his focus at the instrument reminds me of watching him with a camera in his hands
afterwards   m & i walk from my mom's apartment on 26th back to times square

we kiss past the new york public library   into the red light on our
faces of 42nd street
kissing is moving forward through space   kissing is walking kissing
is swimming kissing is
flying
falling

On Christmas day I talk to each of them on the phone, hiding in my
brother's old bedroom in my mom's apartment.
P cries because he drunkenly opened my Nikon, exposing the film
with our last photos together, the ones that were probably too dark to
develop properly anyway. In a day he will move out of our apartment.
He tells me he hooked up with a girl in our bed a few nights before,
while I was with M. Talking to him, I am fucked up, angry, even
though I know it's not really fair. I cry. I feel like I can't breathe. I tell
him I'm sick of playing this tennis game of hurt.
Later, on the phone, M and I recount our strange last hour together,
just a day ago: We said goodbye in front of the hotel / his cab waiting /
he pulled me into the car with him / I told him I am the person I want
to be in his presence / even though we were just fighting / our first
real fight / because he said he doesn't need to call himself a feminist
/ because he already thinks of women as superior to men / I told him
this was stupid / he said I wasn't understanding him / a language
problem / I wasn't sure if it was / but he was leaving and there wasn't
time so we kissed and cried in the cab and he sprayed me all over with
his perfume / as we got closer and closer to the edge of Manhattan /
the edge of my island / and I had to get out / and then he was gone.
In an email P tells me how *The Unbearable Lightness of Being* came
into his mind recently—he'd read it years ago (so had I, though I
didn't remember it well), and the title entered his mind randomly as
if it spoke to this moment. P writes:

I remember liking the main character and his view that sex and
love were two separate concepts. That was about all i remembered

until I went back through the plot today and was like hmmm maybe this book doesnt hold up anymore.

Turns out the guy is just kinda a dick and cheats on his wife all the time and his wife is really unhappy until she finds her true motherly calling raising animals on a farm. Oy books never hold up huh. Also saw that Milan Kundera was a part of trying to get Roman Polanski free. I guess people never really hold up either.

M was reading the book, I tell P. I saw his French copy on the bedside table in New York.

It always takes time for me to adjust, from one to the other. It's not like flipping a switch—now I'm with M, now I'm with P. Each time, there's a slow shift into another way of being with someone, like adjusting to a time change.

In her translator's note for Chantal Akerman's *My Mother Laughs*, Corina Copp writes of a French word she found difficult to properly translate: *The option—whether to use "time difference," "jet lag," maybe "time lag," for décalage—reveals, of course, the interval between one language and another, while décalage means, more theoretically, a "gap" in time or space that allows for a particular voice to construct and, importantly, reconstruct itself. Décalage resists translation and embodies it.* Copp writes that Akerman was *writing, and often suffering, a particular kind of living in the time difference.*

One night in New Orleans, I'm at home by myself. I shave my head, pulling the clippers through thick hair that has grown since M left. Afterward, I admire my stubbled scalp. I'm the only one who can shave my head right.

Recently, a friend—the same one who happened to gift me the book when we graduated from college—coincidentally sent me a quote from *The Unbearable Lightness of Being* in response to my love situation: *There is no means of testing which decision is better, because there is no basis for comparison . . . That is why life is always like a sketch. No, "sketch" is not quite the word, because a sketch is an outline of something, the groundwork for a picture, whereas the sketch that is our life is a sketch for nothing, an outline with no picture.*

Will M ever read this, what I've written about him? From the start he told me he could not understand my relationship with P; he couldn't understand why we shared all the details. Now, I'm not really sure why we did either. But it felt so necessary, to act as if we could control the hurt. Even though I keep finding myself falling in love, I've never thought of myself as a romantic person. I've always been repelled by the gender roles implicit in this game. I've never liked the idea of giving up control in a relationship, especially since I'm a "woman" who typically finds myself involved with "men." Now, I think insisting on the open relationship with P was a way of never letting myself fall too hard, out of fear of losing myself. If I could maintain this particular way of being in the world, being able to flirt with, kiss, even fuck other people, I would never lose control. Until now I did not want to admit that love is losing control. In resisting the fairy tale so adamantly, I lost track of what I was even looking for.

In our Times Square hotel room, M and I smoke a joint late one night and, naked next to each other in bed, our similarly-sized bodies intertwined, I start to feel as if our flesh is made from the same substance. That's weird, I think, and stop myself from saying it aloud to him— wouldn't that mean we were siblings, twins? But still something about the stoned-thought rings true, and for once I want to get lost in the potential cheesiness of it, the *cheesiness* I protected myself from for so long—perhaps it's not a coincidence that for me this word is synonymous with magic. When my skin meets M's, it feels as if it's greeting something familiar.

at a bar called burp castle on 7th where you can only whisper or else the bartender reprimands you   finger to his lips   reverent   m goes to smoke a cigarette outside   i watch through glass

& get a phone call: it's him

we laugh   quietly   talk on the phone   his voice is slightly removed
from the movements of his mouth and i feel like he is so far away
again   in *france* a place of my imagination   reduced to how i've
known him the past month

how i will know him for months to come

i'll tell him our situation reminds me of the movie *her*   of falling in
love with a voice on a phone

in *her*   i love when the os says *the past is just a story we tell ourselves*
her voice full of the

wonder of realization

later she confesses to theodore she's in love with hundreds of
others   *but the heart's not like a box that gets filled up; it expands in
size the more you love . . .*

on the first day in new york m told me he likes girls who other people
don't find attractive and this tugs at me for the four days

now i ask if he meant me and he jokes *yes you look like a little boy and
it's weird*

how much i like this

later he tells me he sees gender as an attribute beyond humanity
every inanimate object in his language   one   or the other
we differ in this perception   i don't know if it's good

in a bar on the upper west side   after walking for hours through
central   later riverside   park   after flying back and forth on the
swings i used to smoke on as a teenager

i see some people i recognize from high school and

tell m i'm writing something about him but can't explain what

he seems a little flattered

a little scared

*You're lucky that you can write your feelings on paper. I want to scream
my love for you at the moment. I should make a film but you know how it
is . . . filmmaking is a long process and I want everything now with you,*
M writes to me a few days after hc left New York and crossed the ocean

again. M says he's corny in English. He thinks he's cleverer, more poetic, in French. Yet, with him, I learn English again. He shows me these old words can still be exciting. One night he messages me out of nowhere: *we should kiss between our sigh.* I don't ask what this means. I don't need to. What if our sighs, our sorrows, could be joined by a kiss?

the first night of 2020 and i'm weeping on the floor after talking to p
on the phone
he told me about his new years eve   when i talked to m at midnight
(6 a.m. his time) and not
p
who was at a big warehouse party   sitting in a metallic womb   on
molly and shrooms   dancing & making out with   a   all over the party
i'm sad to hear about his freeness   when for almost 6 years i had to
drag him out to parties   drag him to the
dance floor
i feel my heart actually break   but finally i'm ready to let the current
take me
i have so much joy in me i tell p
why didn't you want to find it
and you—can you only be free without me
i was scared he says
scared of being myself in public
we were so young
i am still young but i feel old

Alone in my apartment one night—newly *my* apartment—I'm about to get into bed but feel oddly energetic. These days I'm attracted to goofy bedtime rituals, ways to mark the end of the day when there's no one to say goodnight to. I put on a song, a Disney song I secretly love, and blast it like only a crazy person would: "How Far I'll Go" from Moana. The tinkling of wind chimes, a rainstick, signals anticipation before that first line, about her staring out at the edge of the water without understanding why. I sing along with theatrical reverence as I abandon the clothes I've worn all day and pull on my oversized Saints T-shirt. I love how Moana is drawn to the edge, that line where sky and sea meet. I love when she asks if she will cross that line, because as soon as she voices the question we know she will, like Pocahontas following her dreams around the riverbend. In the song Moana explains that, though everyone is happy on the island she's from, she has this itch, this desire she can't control, pulling her out to the unknown. Moana pleads to know what is wrong with her. I laugh at how much delight it brings me to let these words escape my mouth, filling my bedroom with a new sense of life, a life it never contained before, just me and this story.

*

One week into the new year, 2020, I had my final reading for the low-residency writing program I was graduating from. My parents came up from New York to Vermont for the night. They were staying in the same hotel, in separate rooms, and seemed to be getting along, though their combined presence made me nervous. They still could divorce or get back together, and my siblings and I had all been living in this gray area with them for almost four years, the gray area my own relationship had now made a home in. P also came for the reading, flying up from New Orleans—even though he slept with A the night before his flight, even though I was just with M in New York—so he could finally see the world I'd briefly disappeared to every six months for the past two years. He'd bought the tickets before our breakup, and he wanted to meet my friends and professors and see my reading; for some reason I felt unable to tell him he couldn't come. Really, a part of me wanted him there. But I also knew it was wrong because I couldn't bring myself to tell M that P would be there. I couldn't keep this up much longer, the secrets boring a hole inside me that would only continue to grow if I didn't let them escape. My heart would need to pick a time zone.

The night of the reading, I was the last of three readers. My hands began to shake as I put a mug of hot water, lemon, and whiskey to my lips and waited, trying to listen to my friends read, my brain foggy with anticipation. My advisor introduced me, and then I somehow found myself at the podium, saying words I couldn't believe I was saying aloud. During the weeks leading up to this moment, I had been so sure of the essay, that it was the one I should read, but then I was up there in front of so many people, telling them the story—of the hurricane that never came and of how I loved P, of how I wanted to be seen differently by him, of how he had sex with A, of how I too slept with someone else, of how we started to fall apart or, perhaps, had been falling apart all along—and I surprised myself with my honesty. As the room around me melted, I had only the words to cling to and I held onto them with my shaking voice; if I let go, I knew I would fall.

Afterward, my friends congratulated me, and I could finally breathe again. P came to hug me. My friends as well as strangers told me I was brave, for sharing so much. I didn't feel brave. In fact, over and over again, the comment made me feel like I'd violated a social code of how much we are meant to share of ourselves. I always share too much.

My parents congratulated me, but my mom kept saying, *We are the coolest parents ever for sitting through that.* I wasn't sure what she meant—*had she considered getting up and stomping out of the room?* I joked. My dad didn't agree with her, though; he could handle it, he said, and as always I loved him for this. When P was out of hearing distance, my mom told me she was going to buy me a plane ticket to Paris as my graduation gift. She wanted me to see M, to chase M if I had to. I suddenly thought of a Gloria Steinem quote I'd heard years before—*Like so many women, I was living out the unlived life of my mother*—I've always liked this line, but I don't think this is what it means: that our mothers are permitted to live vicariously through our love lives, that our mothers can try to right the wrongs of their own relationships through ours. Still, I thanked her and accepted the gift. I would go to Paris. I would chase M because with him I somehow became my child self again, a little boy/girl with a reckless imagination, and at the same time I could see myself older, could think of the future. I thanked her for coming to the reading, for supporting me, for showing me how to share too much.

A few days after my graduation, during one of our final dinners together, P told me that, though he was glad he came to the reading and was proud of me, I hadn't gotten the story right. He'd read the essay months before but said when he heard it aloud, it was different. He didn't think it was true that he couldn't see me the way I wanted to be seen. I argued with him for a while, about how I was sure he wanted me to be different, more femme or something, because he'd recently gifted me a pair of hoop earrings. I was still holding to this version of the narrative; I continued to embrace the story I had read aloud as the illustration of our main issue. That night he ultimately agreed to my version, probably just to end the fight.

Weeks later P and I were back in New Orleans, living in different apartments but continuing to run into each other around the neighborhood and at parties. One night we were in a group of people outside a bar, and I noticed P talking to another friend and referring to me with a nod, calling me *they*. How long, I wondered, had he been doing this?

I can only write my own truth and, even then, I won't get it right. That's the thing about truth, it's like the delta, like the River when it could move: it's always shifting, changing.

Even as I pick out these details of M for you to look at, I know I'm skewing the reality. I wonder if I'm still trying to find ways to deny what seems impossible: that from the moment we first kissed, *I knew* I loved him. (And, crazier still, that impossibility—the part of me that does believe in it—might actually be the source of my joy).

I will never forget the pain of finding out the truth about my parents, of hearing all the details since our mom never holds anything back. Like my mom I sometimes can't control my honesty even when it hurts. But I'm so scared of the opposite, of pulling the curtain, saying there's nothing to see here, of locking up stories in the vault, especially in art—it reminds me too much of Disney. Maybe that's why I find myself so attracted to the naked truth, why attempting to perform this truth feels like my purest expression of self. I'm not really sure if this is brave, though, or selfish.

Sometimes I want to work a knife through the threads that attach this Disney thing to me, I told M recently, miming the gesture with my hands. *Cut it loose, let it float away into the sky like a cluster of birthday balloons. Maybe that's why you write about it,* he suggested, *when you put the stories on the page, you don't have to hold them anymore.* I was so relieved he understood this: the words can be the sharp tool.

I don't know if M will stick around if he ever reads this.

I hope he will.

Yet, still, I cannot contain myself. I don't know what to do but to try to tell the truth. Especially now, as I fall apart, as I find the joy in falling.

    *

on the lip of the mississippi by myself
on my twenty-ninth birthday   i sit on a rock   water lapping toward
my boots
with a plastic flask of jack daniels
and a freshly shaved scalp
and my journal
and the steamboat natchez floating by on brown water
toward the sharp curve in the River i always find myself drawn to
the sun dropping slowly   i write some sentences   some stories
in my journal
about the swamp where i live
and the island where i grew up

about love
about disorientation
about art
about imagination
sometimes i feel like i'm forever tied up in a love story   not with
a person   but with the
words
& how i try to make sense of my life with them
the truth i attempt to find though know i never will
perhaps i'm in love purely with the desire that pulls me to the edge

acknowledgments

I would like to thank all of those who read this book in its different forms, who gave me feedback and support as it took shape, including my professors at Vermont College of Fine Arts, Trinie Dalton, Harrison Candelaria Fletcher, Anthony Swofford, and Bret Lott, and my good friends and fellow writers Ashley Moore, Beck Kitsis, Sasha Solodukhina, and Katie Hoar.

Big thanks to Sue William Silverman for your mentorship and to my editor Courtney Ochsner. Thank you to Clifford Chase, who first told me I was a writer, to Deborah Kriger and all of my other wonderful professors along the way, including Tomás Q. Morín, Ellen Lesser, and Robert Vivian. Thanks to those who gave me invaluable advice as I sought to publish my first book, Sofia Warren, Caleb Curtiss, Adam McOmber, Jonathan Patten, Elena Passarello, and Brooke Wentz. Thanks to the editors of *Prairie Schooner*, *Crazyhorse*, *Hobart*, the *Writer's Chronicle*, and *Third Coast* for publishing previous versions of some of these pieces. Thanks to fellow filmmakers Kira Akerman and Monique Walton as well as to Annabelle, Tanielma, Kenzie, and the rest of the *Hollow Tree* team, with whom I learned about the control of the River and its echoes in our lives.

Many thanks to all of the writers and filmmakers I've drawn inspiration from and to everyone else who taught me how to imagine / how to love: Mom and Dad; my siblings, Olivia, Henry, and Eamon; Nonna and Ninch; Grandpa and Grandma; my aunts Katie, Sarah, and Susan and my uncles Tim and Roy; the rest of my family, including Maggie and Tim, Leah and Peter, Debbie and Brian, Sophie, Mary, Nasser, John, Leymah, Julia, Bobby, Kevin, Scott, Eleni, Nathaniel, Anastasia, Sarah, Chris, Jean, Jeremy, P, Lauren, Chelsea, Heather, Mike, Bennett, Dea, and Miriam; et Maxime, merci, not only for reminding me of how scared-but-brave I am, but for being a sensitive, crazy, brilliant person who I continually learn from.

Thank you, last but not least, to New Orleans and all of its beautiful inhabitants, without whom I could not have written this book.

notes

THIS SUMMER, HIGH RIVER

1. Redding S. Sugg Jr., ed., *The Horn Island Logs of Walter Inglis Anderson*, rev. ed. (Jackson: University Press of Mississippi, 1985), 126.
2. Susan Buchanan, "Focus on Coastal Restoration Not Retreat, Louisiana's Senator Landrieu Says," *Huffington Post*, last modified May 18, 2012, www.huffpost.com.

THE BOYS WHO WOULDN'T GROW UP

1. Aisha Harris, "Why Is Peter Pan Usually Played by a Woman?" *Slate*, January 23, 2014, slate.com.
2. Sarah Laskow, "The Racist History of Peter Pan's Indian Tribe," *Smithsonian Magazine*, December 2, 2014, www.smithsonianmag.com.
3. "Betty Bronson (1906–1971)," Golden Silents, June 14, 2020, www.goldensilents.com.
4. Robert Vivian, "Please Don't Accuse Me of Genre" (lecture, Vermont College of Fine Arts, Montpelier VT, Summer 2016).

ASHES

1. Erich Schwartzel, "Disney World's Big Secret: It's a Favorite Spot to Scatter Family Ashes," *Wall Street Journal*, October 24, 2018, www.wsj.com.
2. Phoebe Zerwick, "Take Them to the River," *The Bitter Southerner*, bittersoutherner.com.
3. Brooks Barnes, "Roy E. Disney Dies at 79; Rejuvenated Animation," *New York Times*, December 17, 2009, www.nytimes.com.

DISNEYFICATION

1. Jeff Adelson, "Four French Quarter Strip Clubs Allowed to Resume Operations; Earlier Protest Disrupts Tourism Event," *Nola.com*, January 31, 2018, www.nola.com.
2. Peter Dreier and Daniel Flaming, "Op-Ed: Disneyland's Workers Are Undervalued, Disrespected and Underpaid," *Los Angeles Times*, February 28, 2018, www.latimes.com.
3. Kerri Anne Renzulli, "Disney Isn't the Only Company Paying its CEO 1,000 Times More Than Its Typical Employee Earns—Here Are 12 Others," CNBC, last modified April 23, 2019, www.cnbc.com.
4. Brandon Katz, "The Walt Disney Company's Major Recent Acquisitions, Ranked by Cost," *Observer*, September 22, 2020, observer.com.
5. Paulina Velasco, "Cinderella Is Homeless, Ariel 'Can't Afford to Live on Land': Disney under Fire for Pay," *The Guardian*, July 17, 2017, www.theguardian.com.
6. C. J. Lotz, "How New Orleans Inspired Walt Disney," *Garden & Gun*, October 26, 2017, gardenandgun.com.
7. Dave Walker, "Walt Disney and New Orleans: A Visionary and His Muse," *Nola.com*, September 15, 2015, www.nola.com.

IMAGINEERING

1. Margarita Noriega, "Read the Rejection Letters Disney Used to Send Any Woman Who Wanted to Be an Animator," *Vox*, July 16, 2015, www.vox.com.
2. Patricia Zohn, "Coloring the Kingdom," *Vanity Fair*, February 5, 2010, www.vanityfair.com.
3. Matt Singer, "Just How Racist is 'Song of the South,' Disney's Most Notorious Movie?" *ScreenCrush*, last modified March 4, 2016, screencrush.com.
4. Thomas LeClair, "A Conversation with Toni Morrison: The Language Must Not Sweat," *The New Republic*, March 21, 1981, newrepublic.com.
5. John McQuaid, "Chemical Corridor: Black Residents Shoulder the Heaviest Burden of Pollution Along the Mississippi River," *Nola.com*, May 21, 2000, www.nola.com.
6. Leon Waters, Hidden History Tours, New Orleans, www.hiddenhistory.us.
7. Michelle Baran, "Attendance at Disney's Animal Kingdom Surges in 2017," *Travel Weekly*, May 21, 2018, www.travelweekly.com.
8. "Grant Federal Recognition to the United Houma Nation," Petition by Colette Pichon Battle, The Action Network, actionnetwork.org.
9. Adam Crepelle, "Louisiana's Houma Indians Fight for Federal Recognition," *Facing South*, November 29, 2011, www.facingsouth.org.

ROAD TRIP

1. Sally Black, "How Much Does A Disney World Vacation Cost?" Vacation Kids, March 8, 2013, www.vacationkids.com.
2. "Average Domestic Airline Itinerary Fares," Bureau of Transportation Statistics, United States Department of Transportation, www.transtats.bts.gov.
3. Kimberly Amadeo, "What is the Average Income in the United States?" *The Balance*, last modified December 27, 2021, www.thebalance.com.
4. "Carousel of Progress (Magic Kingdom)—Current Version (1994-Present)," *Disney Park Scripts*, September 22, 2015, www.disneyparkscripts.com.
5. The Walt Disney Company, "Epcot/Florida Film," 1966, https://www.youtube.com/watch?v=sLCHg9mUBag&ab_channel=TheOriginalEPCOT.

IN THE AMERICAN LIVES SERIES

The Twenty-Seventh Letter of the Alphabet: A Memoir
BY KIM ADRIAN

Fault Line
BY LAURIE ALBERTS

Pieces from Life's Crazy Quilt
BY MARVIN V. ARNETT

Songs from the Black Chair: A Memoir of Mental Illness
BY CHARLES BARBER

This Is Not the Ivy League: A Memoir
BY MARY CLEARMAN BLEW

Body Geographic
BY BARRIE JEAN BORICH

Driving with Dvořák: Essays on Memory and Identity
BY FLEDA BROWN

Searching for Tamsen Donner
BY GABRIELLE BURTON

Island of Bones: Essays
BY JOY CASTRO

American Lives: A Reader
EDITED BY ALICIA CHRISTENSEN
INTRODUCED BY TOBIAS WOLFF

If This Were Fiction: A Love Story in Essays
BY JILL CHRISTMAN

Get Me Through Tomorrow: A Sister's Memoir of Brain Injury and Revival
BY MOJIE CRIGLER

Should I Still Wish: A Memoir
BY JOHN W. EVANS

Out of Joint: A Private and Public Story of Arthritis
BY MARY FELSTINER

Descanso for My Father: Fragments of a Life
BY HARRISON CANDELARIA FLETCHER

My Wife Wants You to Know I'm Happily Married
BY JOEY FRANKLIN

Weeds: A Farm Daughter's Lament
BY EVELYN I. FUNDA

Falling Room
BY ELI HASTINGS

It's Fun to Be a Person I Don't Know
BY CHACHI D. HAUSER

Borderline Citizen: Dispatches from the Outskirts of Nationhood
BY ROBIN HEMLEY

The Distance Between: A Memoir
BY TIMOTHY J. HILLEGONDS

Opa Nobody
BY SONYA HUBER

*Pain Woman Takes Your Keys, and
Other Essays from a Nervous System*
BY SONYA HUBER

*Hannah and the Mountain: Notes
toward a Wilderness Fatherhood*
BY JONATHAN JOHNSON

Under My Bed and Other Essays
BY JODY KEISNER

*Local Wonders: Seasons
in the Bohemian Alps*
BY TED KOOSER

A Certain Loneliness: A Memoir
BY SANDRA GAIL LAMBERT

Bigger than Life: A Murder, a Memoir
BY DINAH LENNEY

What Becomes You
BY AARON RAZ LINK
AND HILDA RAZ

*Queen of the Fall: A Memoir
of Girls and Goddesses*
BY SONJA LIVINGSTON

*The Virgin of Prince Street:
Expeditions into Devotion*
BY SONJA LIVINGSTON

*Anything Will Be Easy after This:
A Western Identity Crisis*
BY BETHANY MAILE

Such a Life
BY LEE MARTIN

Turning Bones
BY LEE MARTIN

In Rooms of Memory: Essays
BY HILARY MASTERS

Island in the City: A Memoir
BY MICAH MCCRARY

Between Panic and Desire
BY DINTY W. MOORE

*To Hell with It: Of Sin and Sex,
Chicken Wings, and Dante's
Entirely Ridiculous, Needlessly
Guilt-Inducing "Inferno"*
BY DINTY W. MOORE

Let Me Count the Ways: A Memoir
BY TOMÁS Q. MORÍN

Shadow Migration: Mapping a Life
BY SUZANNE OHLMANN

*Meander Belt: Family, Loss,
and Coming of Age in the
Working-Class South*
BY M. RANDAL O'WAIN

Sleep in Me
BY JON PINEDA

*The Solace of Stones: Finding
a Way through Wilderness*
BY JULIE RIDDLE

Works Cited: An Alphabetical Odyssey of Mayhem and Misbehavior
BY BRANDON R. SCHRAND

Thoughts from a Queen-Sized Bed
BY MIMI SCHWARTZ

My Ruby Slippers: The Road Back to Kansas
BY TRACY SEELEY

The Fortune Teller's Kiss
BY BRENDA SEROTTE

Gang of One: Memoirs of a Red Guard
BY FAN SHEN

Just Breathe Normally
BY PEGGY SHUMAKER

How to Survive Death and Other Inconveniences
BY SUE WILLIAM SILVERMAN

The Pat Boone Fan Club: My Life as a White Anglo-Saxon Jew
BY SUE WILLIAM SILVERMAN

Scraping By in the Big Eighties
BY NATALIA RACHEL SINGER

Sky Songs: Meditations on Loving a Broken World
BY JENNIFER SINOR

In the Shadow of Memory
BY FLOYD SKLOOT

Secret Frequencies: A New York Education
BY JOHN SKOYLES

The Days Are Gods
BY LIZ STEPHENS

Phantom Limb
BY JANET STERNBURG

This Jade World
BY IRA SUKRUNGRUANG

The Sound of Undoing: A Memoir in Essays
BY PAIGE TOWERS

When We Were Ghouls: A Memoir of Ghost Stories
BY AMY E. WALLEN

Knocked Down: A High-Risk Memoir
BY AILEEN WEINTRAUB

Yellowstone Autumn: A Season of Discovery in a Wondrous Land
BY W. D. WETHERELL

This Fish Is Fowl: Essays of Being
BY XU XI

To order or obtain more information on these or other University of Nebraska Press titles, visit nebraskapress.unl.edu.